RAINBOW
FARM

Robert R. Williams

PAGE PUBLISHING, INC.
Conneaut Lake, PA

First originally published by Page Publishing 2019

ISBN 978-1-64584-979-7 (pbk)
ISBN 978-1-64701-080-5 (hc)
ISBN 978-1-64584-980-3 (digital)

Printed in the United States of America

ACKNOWLEDGEMENTS

The author would like to express his gratitude to Page Publishing and especially Holly Ickes his Publication Coordinator for her professionalism and support in publishing his first work. It was all new for me but Holly's assistance and guidance were a huge part of this publication coming to fruition. I would also like to express my thanks and gratitude to Deborah Perdue and Illumination Graphics and her artist Tara Thelen for her phenomenal work on the illustrations for Rainbow Farm. It was Tara whose talent brought these characters to life and for that I am truly grateful.

I would greatly appreciate hearing from readers at
robertrwilliamsauthor@gmail.com

CHAPTER 1

The Big Three

CAM, PETE, AND SHRILL

All was not well on the most popular estate in all the land known as Rainbow Farm. Recognized for its diversity of terrain and species, Rainbow was the farm around the world that animals from all over wanted to join. Many of the animals had become hopelessly separated over time and were hopelessly bickering due to a plethora of issues and differences. As a result, the barnyard had been divided up into parcels premised upon ideologies where animals could hang out in proverbial safe spaces. These parcels basically amounted to echo chambers where animals could hold their little rallies and go unchallenged spewing their partisan views. This was nothing new, and there had been differences in the past between the two parties: the Donkeys, sometimes referred to as the Asses, and the other party, the Elephants. However, this time, it seemed more divided. There was no crossing over and breaking bread with those on the other side and attempt at negotiations on even the simplest of issues. Many moons ago, a former leader had said, "A house divided cannot stand." Is this where the farm was headed?

At the center of the barnyard was a white barn where the Chief of the Farm, known as the CoF, resided and ruled over this hopelessly divided mob. That animal was Cam, a chameleon lizard that possessed the uncanny ability to change his colors to match whatever color would symbolically match the situation. With much fanfare and audacity of hope, and as a left-leaning member of the Donkey party, he had ruled the roost for over seven-plus years and was nearing the end of his rule as the next CoF election was scheduled later that year. Cam's administration had begun with much hope and promise and fanfare. He was the first lizard ever elected to the position and promised complete transparency and better times to come. Cam was never seen without his trademark, a red pen. It was purely symbolic and void of any ink. Once in reaction to a dispute on a neighboring farm Cam had intervened and stated, "I will not tolerate state-sponsored vermin on the other farm who terrorize their fellow farm animals by putting rat poison in their food stores." Whipping out his trademark pen and changing his skin color to bright red for added effect, he then said, "This is my red line. I will not tolerate such atrocious behavior." As the carnage continued and Cam never did anything, the joke was that his coveted red pen had no ink, his so-called red lines were invisible and crossed frequently without any impunity. Still, he carried around the pen like a badge of honor.

Cam had also pushed programs regarding health care for all the animals on the farm. "You can keep your vets," he promised. Well, it didn't really turn out that way. Like any other hot-button issue, this was one that animals either hated or loved. The problem with these overarching policies is that certain areas and animals they suited well, and others they did not. A compromise would have been to leave this to local jurisdictions, but that ship had sailed, and the result was just one more contentious log added to the fire of divide. Cam had also upset many of the animals when he provided large stores of grain to the Oil Farm. This farm had been recognized by many administrations prior to Cam's as an enemy of their farm. For years, assets from the enemy farm had been held, and now Cam felt the time was right to bury the hatchet. Many disagreed. This farm had been behind many acts of vandalism on several farms and was a sworn enemy of the Rainbow Farm. Why give them anything that in any way would sustain their illegal activities?

Cam was a difficult read. Even though the hawks on the farm were displeased with payments to the Oil Farm, he was also quite draconian when need be. This Jekyll-Hyde approach involved him reaching out in very benevolent fashion with one hand and using secret military operations to settle scores with the other. For those who characterized him as a dove, they were proven wrong time and time again. He may appear soft, but behind the scenes, he used all the tools on the farm to reach out and punish those who did the Rainbow Farm harm even if that meant going after his own animals wherever they may be, whether hiding out on the farm as well as off the farm. One of the most celebratory moments of Cam's administration was the takedown of a rogue camel named Laddy. This despicable creature, who was the mastermind behind an attack on the farm years earlier had been enemy number one of the entire Rainbow Farm for years. Laddy had sent undercover camels onto Rainbow Farm who were responsible for mass destruction and loss of life of thousands of innocent animals. Outstanding work and surveillance by the intelligence community located Laddy on a farm in Land of the Stans. Cam then gave the green light for condors loaded down with wolverines to go over and execute Laddy in what was known as Operation Take Down the Camel. Mission was accomplished, Laddy was exterminated, and the Rainbow Farm was celebrated. In an iconic photo, one gets a glimpse into how cool, calm, and collected Cam could be. In the photo, Cam is standing at the table watching the operation in real time. He is surrounded by his staff to include Ed the Toad, Caesar the Orangutan, Shrill the Parrot looking scared with her claw on her beak, and his deputy Sniffy the Hound. What a proud moment for Cam as his colors shifted back in forth to red, white, and blue and all colors of the Rainbow Farm. He proudly stroked his worldly medal he had won for bringing peace throughout the land and tapped his red pen on the desk.

On the lighter side, Cam had many qualities that appealed to all animals. Regardless of if one voted for Cam or not, one could not help but appreciate his ability to be cool. He could croon, was an excellent speaker, and had a mean game of hoops. Cam was a polarizing figure. Those animals who voted for him were sycophants who refused to criticize him when he was obviously wrong, and those animals who did not vote for him were incapable of resisting character assassination just because they did not agree with his policies. Such was the quagmire called the Rainbow Farm. A polarized electorate who refused all compromise, a model of efficiency it was not.

Take that nasty camel!

Shrill and Pete

For the upcoming election, there was a perennial favorite among Cam's party, the Donkeys, and it was Shrill. She was a seasoned candidate with tons of name recognition, and as Cam was the first lizard ever elected to office, she was also destined to be a first as the first female parrot to ever hold the office of CoF. In addition to her long list of accomplishments and political experience, she was entering the race with significant baggage. A hot-blooded bird with an attitude who got things done would be a fair description. But her fiery personality and disposition also had a downside. Shrill was prone to sudden outbursts of anger and once had been rumored to have thrown the garden ax at her husband, Rex the Rooster, when he was caught red-handed in the chicken coop courting numerous young hens. Despite her obvious character flaws, she was the front runner, and in her and several other's opinions, it was her turn to be at the helm. It was destiny. She was preordained. The glass ceiling would be shattered. Balloons would fall, and she would soon rule. The only competition in her party to challenge her for the Donkey's nomination was an aged bear known as Old Red whose fur always looked as if it was combed with a balloon. Rumor had it he had once visited the Red Farm on his honeymoon and never returned. However, Old Red would give her a run for her money as there was an awakening of sorts, a grassroots movement of younger animals from the far left, who were totally buying what Old Red was selling. It would be a battle between the two for the Donkey nomination.

In the other party, the Elephants, candidates were lining up to run and consisted of the usual suspects to include a low-energy sloth named Sleepy and a combination of many different creatures. There was a buzz in the air as it was rumored that a well-known businessman, Pete the Peacock, was considering entering the race. No one believed he would really get in as he had expressed interest before but never followed through. All believed he would remain on the business side of things heavily involved in his company known for building towers on the Rainbow farm as well as foreign farmyards across the land. Imagine the shock and surprise followed by laughter when a coach pulled up, and Pete wearing a red hat atop his orange plume with the letters MFGA along with his beautiful wife, a foreign-born beautiful swan named Lena descended the golden stairs. "I have an announcement," crowed Pete.

"What's with the hat?" asked Kyle the King Snake. "What does MFGA stand for?"

Pete replied, "It stands for Make Farm Grow Again. I am here to make things great again and my first order of business will be to build a new fence around the barnyard. No longer will the other animals from neighboring farms be able to come into our barnyard without proper documentation. I'm gonna bring jobs and prosperity back to this farm, I'm gonna make it safe again, I'm gonna make it fertile again, and I'm gonna make it grow again."

So the stage was set, and it would be the Peacock going against well-established politicians gunning for the Elephant Party's nomination to become the Chief of the Farm. All the animals on both sides howled with laughter. Ridicule and disbelief went all the way to the top as Cam had a drop the mic moment ridiculing Pete as someone who would never be CoF. Members of the Elephant party especially the Rhinoceros Club did not give him a chance and were in silent opposition. Once Pete crossed that line and entered their world, it was game on. None of the establishment liked him, none supported him, and everyone said he had no chance to win. But Pete didn't care. Assisted by his numbers guy, the bearded stork, he knew something that the entire establishment did not. The entire congregation of just regular animals on the farm were sick of both parties, Elephants and Donkeys alike. They wanted change, and Pete was their guy. After all, Pete had accomplished things; he was a builder. The animals on the farm could see his towers from afar on other farms, and they seemed to be buying what Pete was selling. At one time, it was Cam stressing the importance of big government that told the animals when referring to infrastructure. "You did not build this."

Pete just grinned and pointed at one of his many towers. "Yes, I did build that." The animals were hungry for a builder and a doer; they had heard enough talk from previous administrations to include Donkeys and Elephants.

On the other side, Shrill didn't seem to care about Pete getting in the race. She and the rest of the Donkeys were convinced she had it in the bag. The first hurdle would be disposing of the tired, old, disheveled bear Old Red. This should be easy; after all, she was the establishment. She had no shortage of funding, as animals all over the world were convinced she would be the next CoF and donated large sums of money to her campaign. This was normal practice as all animals were placing bets on who would win and donations to a candidate—in this case, Shrill—rolled in because donors were hoping to have favors returned once she won. Besides, she had the support of Cam. In a secret agreement and pact made long ago, Cam had promised his support to Shrill breaking from tradition and not supporting his vice as a candidate an old hound dog known as Sniffy. There really was no way she could lose. It was a done deal; she intended to secure the Donkey nomination and whoever the Elephants selected as their party nominee she would dispatch of easily. A third administration of Cam via proxy Shrill was inevitable.

In the days and months following Pete's ceremonious announcement, the momentum spiked. His catchy phrases of "Build that Fence!" and "Make Farm Grow Again!" could be heard loud and proud at the numerous rallies he conducted throughout the barnyard. Everywhere he went throughout the barnyard, massive groups of excited animals would gather just to see and hear Pete make his case as a candidate. "He's one of us." "He cares about us." "He's gonna build a fence." Pete went throughout the entire farm, promising to get rid of big government and rescind regulations that had been a thorn in the side of the animals for years. He promised to reduce taxes and create more jobs, a four-letter word, not three. He promised to control the influx of new animals into the farm and to put the farm first. He promised new infrastructure and a stronger barnyard protection force. He was becoming quite the politician adept at telling the animals what they wanted to hear. Unlike Cam and Shrill, he came across more authentic. He never altered the inflection of his voice to fit into a certain group. He never mooed like a cow; he never oinked like a pig. He was a peacock and spoke with the same accent every time. Nothing phony about Pete—what you saw is what you got, and at every rally he dressed the same, always sharp with his open jacket and long red tie. What a sight, the peacock all flashy and looking good standing knee deep in a pig sty. Pete would close out the energy-filled sessions with his closing comments of "We're gonna make the farm *safe* again, we're gonna make the farm *fertile* again, and we're gonna *make farm grow again!*" with background music from a famous Limey Band known as the Stationary Rocks.

The Campaign and Debates

In addition to the rallies there was debates. Oh, how Pete shined in the debates. His beautiful orange hue and plume made him stand out among the rest of the candidates. Very early on, everyone recognized Pete had the "it" factor and not one political bone in his body and that resonated because they were sick of politicians. The debates took place in the center of the farmyard. Single stones would be laid out to function as a stand, and according to polling, the higher number you had, the bigger the stone and closer to the center you would be. From the very beginning, Pete occupied the highest perch front and center, and there he would remain. Although designed to discuss serious issues, these debates would very quickly turn into bashing sessions. Pete showed the crowd he was an effective counterpuncher. Not bound by norms and standards of days gone by, he would say anything to anyone and the crowd loved it. If a moderator got sideways with Pete, they paid. If a fellow candidate made fun of the size of his claws, he paid. If someone down the line on the lower end of the debate stage attacked Pete, he reminded them where they currently stood in the queue and labeled them as low energy. The Sloth was his favorite target. Although the Sloth had once been chief executive of a region known as the Glades and his brother had once been CoF, it did not faze Pete. It was his time.

Shrill was not experiencing the easy path she expected. Old Red was giving her a run for her money. One might say there were four parties now: the traditional Elephants and Donkeys and two new ones spurned on by a new wave of populism, Old Red's Red Party and Pete's followers, known as the Deplorables (a moniker laid on them by Shrill that they gladly embraced). For a while, it looked like it might come to a race between Pete and Old Red, but through a rigged system of awarding super corn stalks, Shrill pulled out a squeaker and won the Donkey Primary (awarding corn stalks to the candidates in the primaries was the system utilized to determine the party's winner). Shrill had a history of polarizing and dividing people. Many years ago, when her husband, Rex, had been a chief executive of the farm's diamond mines, she routinely came across as demeaning, condescending, and well—in a nutshell—shrill, how she got her name. So the stage was set. It would be Shrill, the perennial favorite of the establishment, running against Pete, the favorite of the animals.

CHAPTER 2

History, Political Landscape and Geography of Rainbow Farm

The Rainbow Farm was one of the youngest farms on the planet. Although it had not been around as long, it had become the most powerful farm in the world. Because of its size and prosperity, its standing in the group of farms was at the top. It had the most crops, was the most successful, and its diversity earned it the nickname the Melting Pot. Just outside one of its gates was a statue of a giant Mother Hen. Her message inscribed on the base was "Your huddled masses yearning to breathe free, the wretched refuse of your teeming shore. Send these, the homeless, tempest-tost to me. I lift my lamp beside the golden door, come to the Rainbow Farm, be honest, work hard and find your pot of gold." Over the years, several groups of new species had arrived to find their place on the farm and become citizens. Lizards from Limey Farm, frogs from the Frog farm, pandas from the Yellow Farm, burrows from the Brown Farm and other immigrants from all other farms. Some like the black lions had come to the farm involuntary from the Black Farm but, through hard work and perseverance, had become one of the major success stories of the farm.

There were three co-equal branches of government on the farm. An executive, the Chief of Farm, a legislative law-making body composed of two chambers higher and lower, and a judicial branch of nine judges which functioned as the highest court in the land. This system had worked well for the farm over the years, an effective system of coequal branches that were separate but equal. However, over time, certain chiefs had discovered ways of marginalizing the other branches by issuing executive orders. Many animals felt these were royal in nature and in effect like decrees or edicts issued by a king but seemed only to protest when such executive orders did not fit their desires. Normally, these were partisan in nature and issued by a chief who knew he did not have the required numbers for support of his initiative in the legislative chambers to get his ideas across the finish line into law.

"Foul!" would cry the Elephants if a Donkey CoF issued a directive.

"Foul!" would cry the Donkeys if an Elephant CoF issued a directive.

"Needed to be done and what's best for all the animals," brayed the donkeys if a Donkey CoF issued a directive.

"Needed to be done and what's best for all the animals," honked the Elephants if an Elephant CoF issued a directive. The hypocrisy was on full display by both sides. The downside of such executive orders is they were not carved in stone. Whenever a chief from a different party than the previous administration assumed office, the first order of business would be undoing all these executive orders of his predecessor.

THE AGENCIES

Like any government over time, there is a natural evolution where lean and mean becomes bloated and inefficient. In early days, most Rainbow Farm animals worked in the private sector with a very small percentage working for the government. In the past, these select few who penned and passed laws lived most of the time among their constituents where they were able to experience firsthand the impact of such legislation. That had changed over time where these elected officials lived away from their constituents and seem more involved in state matters as opposed to issues that would impact and improve the lives of the public sector. They were omnipresent elite living in echo chambers where they just listened and spoke to each other separated from reality where those who voted them in lived a much different life, one of less privilege and more hardship. The result was that there soon emerged a continental divide between the public and their elected officials. The area where the ruling class congregated became known as the Rancid Pond and was soon the brunt of many jokes. One of those jokes told by a hardworking mole miner one day to his buddy raccoon from the welding shop:

MOLE: Hey you know how many Elephants and Donkeys work at the Rancid Pond?
RACOON: Not sure, how many?
MOLE: A third of them.

Another one was as follows:

MOLE: Why did Mr. Smith go to the Rancid Pond?
RACOON: Not sure why?
MOLE: To find his representative, saw his face on a milk carton, hadn't seen him in years.

Over time, more and more of these organizations emerged with increasing impacts on every facet of the animal's lives. There was a department for this and a department for that. Near the White Barn was where these organizations set up shop enforcing the rules and regulations mandated by the Chief and Congress and High Court. Several of these organizations were involved in gathering intelligence. One was the agency known as the Farmyard Bureau of Investigative Services, FBIS and was led by a gangly giraffe known as Arrogantgit Clouds, AC for short. His name derived from his arrogance and the fact he was so tall his head always seemed to be in the clouds. He fancied himself quite the intelligent one. Tall, handsome, and important was a great way to go through life.

Another responsible for spying on foreign farms was the Central Inflammatory Agency, CIA. Their leader a toad frog named Ed Bighead II, just Ed for short, was known for his red affiliations from days gone by and was a simple-minded creature, who through riding coattails had somehow found his way to one of the highest positions on the farm. Physically, Toad was a perfect fit appearance wise for the CIA; he was the *I* in CIA always looking afflicted and inflamed with something. He seemed to always have a bad disposition and appeared constipated. Always cruel, petty, bossy, with a terrible temper. One had to wonder why one had to be so miserable or at least look that way. "Smile," they would say to Ed. But he never did and appeared to remain in a constant state of grouchiness.

The animal responsible for all these agencies, the director, was an orangutan known as Caesar. He was well-respected and had held various positions on the farm. He was named after a famous chimp who was the smartest of his species and chosen to lead them to freedom and out of captivity from a subspecies known as humans. Caesar's position was relatively new and created shortly after the attack on the farm by Laddy's gang. The idea was this billet would foster more information sharing and coordination between all the agencies. Dealing with enemies foreign and domestic was the primary mission of the CIA and FBI, and Caesar would be the head of this trio working closely with Ed and AC, ensuring the very important business of protecting the farm would be priority number one. What lengths and depths they would go in pursuit of such an important mission was yet to come.

THE EGGTORIAL COLLEGE

A little more on the political landscape of the farm and the system designed by the Founding Animals of the farm to select a Chief of Farm. The fathers realized that the farm would be comprised of different areas with different characteristics. Some like the Hen House were more populated than others such as the cow and horse pastures and meadows. The founding fathers wanted a system where all inhabitants from all areas of the farm would have a say in who would be their leader. According to their written charter, the Almanac, the farm would be a republic and not a democracy. The difference between democracy and republic as a former high judge espoused was the difference between order and chaos. The Founding Animals expressed contempt for the tyranny of majority rule and throughout the Almanac had implemented language stating such. So a system was designed to thwart majority rule when selecting a CoF. This system was called the Eggtorial College. Obtain most of the coveted eggs, 270, and you win, simple as that. Some would say less populated areas of the farm had disproportionate weight compared to more populated areas. Yes, and there was a reason. This system ensured that all areas on the farm to include the hog sty, mole tunnels, pastures, meadows, and ponds had skin in the game when it came to the General Election. If run as a republic and not a democracy, the hen house and other more populated areas of the farm would not be able to bully the more densely populated areas of the farm. This system had served the farm well since its very beginning and was only contested when a candidate won the popular vote but lost the election. The Almanac is there for everyone to read. It's not a secret charter. Begs the question, is it ignorance or contempt of the Almanac that has these sore losers calling to abolish the Eggtorial College?

The physical layout of the farm working from the southwestern portion in a clockwise manner to the northwest corner and then due east across the northern portion over to the northeastern corner then due south to the southeastern corner then due west across the southern portion back to the start point was such: on the southwestern side of the farm was the very populated section consisting of the hen house, golden bears, and mountain lions. Moving up that border, you encountered a duck pond with a healthy population of beavers and above that an apple grove. Moving east from there across the northern portion was a potato farm, followed by grasslands, a dairy farm, and several large catfish ponds. Working south from there was a lobster pond followed by a turtle colony, and then a grove of palmetto trees with gamecock houses and finally ending at a gator pond surrounded by orange trees in the southeast portion. Working west from there across the southern portion of the farm was a crayfish pond followed by a herd of steers. Right next to that was a flock of bighorn sheep, roadrunners, and horny toads in what was once the home to a cantankerous old horned frog known as Gila who once had run for CoF himself. Within the boundaries and the interior of this very diverse landscape were belts originating on the outskirts of the farm and extending inward to its interior confines. There was the Egg Belt, Pork Belt, Dairy Belt, Beef Belt, Fruit Belt, and Leaf Belt. The animals in these respective belts tended to vote a certain way and for a certain type of candidate but not always. Some of these could possibly switch allegiance from one general election to another and were known as Swing Belts.

So no wonder that such a diverse group of species and their specific characteristics and behavior was referred to by many as a melting pot. This arrangement had worked for years somehow, always coming together as one when faced with existential threats and fighting a common enemy. It was during periods of relative peace that problems attributed to the differences between the groups would lead to squabbles many times over the most mundane of issues. These spikes of tension seem to be especially heightened every four years during election cycles. Putting aside that they had more in common than what they disagreed on, the Donkeys and the Elephants would withdrawal to their respective political corners, and the mud-slinging would begin. It was many seasons past when at a critical part of their existence when they were down to only two to each species, a male and a female and being cognizant of the fragility of their situation had bonded together to ensure the perseverance of each other's existence. Shortly after leaving the big ship, it was the elephant with his long snout that pulled a chicken from near death when it was trapped in quicksand. Returning the favor, it was the chicken with a spur to the Elephant's leg that startled the elephant into alertness and moving just in time from the same location where a falling boulder would land seconds later. And these were just two examples of how they had set aside differences and would come together when facing adversity.

But that was a long time ago and over time as their numbers increased and dependency on other species decreased the innate clannish tendencies materialized to the point where they could rely less on the group writ large and more on those who looked like them and thought like them. The farm morphed into echo chambers where like minds and philosophies would reside. Over time, they would basically split into two groups, called parties known as the Donkeys and the Elephants. There were smaller groups, but they paled in comparison to these two main groups and since the existence of the farm it was these two major parties that would hold the highest office of the land. This was an interesting point in time because for the last sixteen years the Elephants and Asses had evenly shared the CoF position. Split into two eight-year time frames beginning with the Elephants and ending with Cam's last term as leader of the Donkeys, the farm was now at a crossroads. Which way would it go? A win for Shrill and basically a third term of Cam policies, or a win for Pete and the ushering in of a businessman, a non-politician.

Both sides took very ridiculous positions of challenging the other side's patriotism and loyalty to the farm, which without contributions from both sides would never have risen to the position of high esteem that it was known for throughout the world. Sally the Hen would say to a deplorable hog, "All you do is wallow around in your sty and eat watermelon rinds."

Arnold the pig would reply, "You sit inside a nice house with your friends, and all you do is cluck all day about nonsense and occasionally lay a few eggs."

Many on the left side of the political spectrum would champion diversity and croon, "Hey it's cool to be different," just one small caveat if you're different just like me. The hypocrisy from both sides was comical. On the right, there would be huge rallies protesting the renaming of certain landmarks and removal of statues. It seemed everyone wanted change if that change suited them and screwed the other side. There was simply no room for compromise.

CHAPTER 3

Frankie, Woo, Rex, Lovebirds, and the Hammer

FRANKIE SEARCHES OUT WOO

Observing this charade perched high above on a limb extending from a towering oak tree dead center of the barnyard was a wise old owl known to all simply as the Wise Old Owl, WOO for short. He had been around for many years having previously served in positions of high authority. He was aware of the political landscape having seen all these shenanigans played out before. For the time being, he just sat on his perch and observed. There may come a day when he would be approached and asked for his opinions, but for now, he just remained quiet, watching and analyzing the charades within the yard. Perched high above the fray, he was viewed as the voice of reason and objectivity at a time when civility was a scarce commodity.

That day arrived one day when Frankie the Praying Mantis came to pay a visit. He was the unofficial leader of a group of very religious and socially conservative animals who were up for grabs as a voting block that most assumed would never vote for a philanderer and cad like Pete, who had been married many times, had several girlfriends and accused of horrible things. Frankie had followed the path of his father Billy who had previously been the top evangelical representative of all the religious animals. Conflicted as to how he should encourage his followers to vote, he decided he would go visit WOO for some advice. Frankie was determined, and it was a long arduous climb to the top limb of the towering oak where WOO hung out. Once reaching the top limb, he very carefully approached WOO.

WOO: Don't worry. I was expecting you. You are the first that has come to seek my counsel. Let me guess, you have reservations about voting for Pete.

FRANKIE: How did you know?"

WOO: There is a large group of you. I call you closet Pete supporters.

FRANKIE: Closet Pete supporters?

WOO: Yes, Closet Pete supporters. Let me explain. You know Pete is the right person to vote for, but you are embarrassed to let everyone else know. But your case is different because your flock looks to you for guidance on who you think is the right choice, so you must publicly make the case. You yourself, Frankie, preach that judge not and you shall not be judged, that let the first one to cast a stone be of no sin, or how you should not throw stones in a glass house. Do you believe in redemption, a fresh start, that despite one's transgressions an animal can be reborn, have a fresh start, do good things for all animals. Isn't that in the realm of the possible? Your group forgave Rex. He spent all his spare time in the Hen House, yet you were able to forgive him. Despite Rex's peccadillos, he was a very good Chief of Farm and loved and respected throughout the land. The other thing to take into consideration is the highest court of the land. Whoever wins the general election will have selection of one, two, maybe three of those judges. Who do you want to make that selection realizing that these are lifetime appointments and will define the political rulings of that body for potentially generations. And this is just a drop in the bucket, there will be hundreds more appointments at lower levels. So get on board with your candidate of choice, and if that requires holding your nose and voting then so be it.

Frankie was enthralled by WOO's words, and suddenly things were becoming clearer. He recollected the verse in the good book, "Judge not and you shall not be judged."

WOO continued, "Let me present you with a scenario, Frankie." WOO looked Frankie directly in the eye and said, "Imagine there is a plane you must fly on. The Plane is named the Rainbow Farm and will transport every single animal and species on the farm to a new location much like Noah did many years ago. There are only two pilots capable of flying the plane. One is Shrill, and the other is Pete. The vote is cast, and regardless who wins and is the pilot of the plane, I ask you…" WOO paused and looked very seriously at Frankie. "Do you want that pilot to be successful?"

FRANKIE: Why of course!
WOO: Then my advice to you is vote for the person who you want to be pilot but if the other one wins by all means be a good passenger on the plane, wish for their success because in the end, every passenger on the Rainbow Farm, regardless of the pilot, should want that pilot to have a safe and successful flight. Understood?

Frankie left that day with a much clearer vision on who he would vote for and went back to his flock and locked down most of their votes for Pete.

Go onward Christian soldier and lock down those votes

REX

As the campaign season progressed, Rex was getting worried. One day, he confronted Shrill. "Get out of the Hen House and go visit Arnold and his friends. You are just remaining in your comfort zone and wasting time on votes you already have." Shrill and her team just laughed off Rex, ignoring the fact he had been elected twice as CoF and was one of the most popular animals on the farm and throughout the lands abroad.

"Oh, Rex," sighed Shrill, "they just love me in the Hen House. Besides, you spend a lot of time in there." She gave a menacing stare. "Why are you giving me such a hard time?"

"And besides," chimed in Tookie, Shrill's young campaign manager, "times have changed, Rex. It's not about just knocking on doors. It's all about collecting data. Your time has passed."

Rex persisted, "You gotta get dirty, get in the Pork Belt, and become recognizable all over the farm. You will rule over all the animals. They need to know you, Shrill." Tookie and Shrill just laughed off Rex and his advice. After all, he was a thing of the past, a relic. They were about the future. But one thing Rex knew from experience, elections were about addition and subtraction, and alienating voters for whatever reason pushed them into the minus column.

A little more on Rex. He was commonly referred to as one of the most brilliant politicians of his lifetime. Smart enough to read the landscape and savvy enough to know where and when to migrate on the political spectrum he was simply brilliant. Love him or hate him for whatever reasons you could not deny the fact he possessed the wow factor. Despite his shortcomings, it was hard to fathom how Shrill and her minions could disregard Rex. Obviously, Shrill never learned anything from Rex. Perhaps she was too busy throwing things at him instead of picking his brain. Regardless of where he went on the farm, he commanded respect. He was also talented as a musician. Many quiet nights on the farm, you could hear Rex playing his saxophone perhaps signaling the hen house that Shrill was out of sight and out of mind, and he, Rex, would be coming over shortly. Despite all his accomplishments as a leader and CoF Rex was, after all, a man, prone to peccadillos, and it would be not a devil in a blue dress that did him in but a young hen in a blue dress named Mo that would be his downfall. Oh, the trials and tribulations of being a banty rooster in the farmyard.

Chicks dig the sax!

Nova and Mona

Love birds Casanova, Nova for short, and Mona were in head over heels in love. As the election neared, Mona's stress level went up. "It looks like Pete will win" she said. "Don't worry," said Nova. "We have an insurance policy." It was obvious these two were anti-Peters. Once in a flyby of the hog pen, Nova was quoted as saying, "I can just smell the Pete supporters, the smell of bacon, mud, and stench." In Nova's mind, he would do everything he could to keep Pete from winning. Both Nova and Mona worked for one of the many intelligence agencies on the farm charged with investigating all crimes within the boundaries of the farm.

THE HAMMER

The Chief of Interior Farm Security, CIFS, a German shepherd, was becoming concerned about the safety of the farm. One night, a very dark night, with zero lunar illumination he was making his nightly rounds and heard a strange clanking noise of what sounded like someone repeatedly hitting something metallic with some sort of blunt object. The commotion was near Shrills Headquarters in a group of trees. What he couldn't see was a tiny mouse named J. C., one of Rex's aides, who, having dragged a hammer into the underbrush, was now mustering his strength to raise the mallet and destroy all the material on the handys.

Oddly enough the next morning, it was the laundry lady who reported several gallons of bleach as being stolen from her washroom. "What in God's creation was going on?" Also, the maintenance man, Marcellus, a razorback, reported missing his hammer, conspicuous because of the stenciled *MINE* on the handle. Perhaps the missing hammer may explain to some degree what the previous night's commotion was all about. One thing is for sure, things were not going to be business as usual in the Pete vs. Shrill show. It was going to get ugly and remain ugly. Hammers and bleach were just peanuts compared to what was to come.

CHAPTER 4

Rex Inspires Pete

One late night on the trail, as Pete was headed to a diner, he ran into of all animals, Rex.

PETE: Rex, Fancy meeting you here, all alone and unafraid.
            Can I join you?

What followed was one of those rare moments, when perceived adversaries set all differences aside and engage in small talk that would eventually become serious. There was no grandstanding, no cameras, just these two blokes who had somehow slipped by their respective security details and wandered around the farm like normal animals.

REX: Sure Pete, have a seat.
PETE: What on God's green earth has you out at this hour?
REX: [*with a sheepish grin*] I was out doing some campaigning
            for Shrill at the hen house and now headed back home.
            Yourself?
PETE: I just needed to escape all the hoopla and just wanted to
            be normal for a second.
REX: Those moments will be few and far between my friend.
            If you beat Shrill, and you just might, your life will never
            be the same.

PETE: How so, can you share with me what it was like living in the White Barn, holding the office and all that goes with that?

REX: Sure, in my second term as Chief, I was out walking one day, and this eagle seemed to be following me. At first, I thought it was Shrill possibly having me tailed but she quit doing that a long time ago. We have an unspoken agreement now where I do my thing and she does hers. To be honest, the only reason she really stuck with me and stood by me like Tammy sings in her song "Stand by Your Man" was for her own political ambition. I would be her ticket to another gig in the White Barn except this time I would be the First Man. What hurts me personally is that after getting her to this point where she has an excellent shot at winning the general election her and her quirky little campaign manager will not even take my advice. You're old Rex. So yesterday, Rex. That's not how it's done these days, Rex. We got this, Rex, please don't embarrass us. Can you believe that, me as one of the most beloved chiefs of all time who won two elections is washed up? I tell her over and over, "Get out of your comfort zone, Shrill. Go see the pigs, Shrill. Be nice to the moles, Shrill. Basically, be kind to your web-footed friend, Shrill. That duck may be someone's mother and she and all her family can vote.

Pete could not believe that Rex was letting his guard down like this and let him continue. After all, they had a lot in common, these two, and Pete genuinely like Rex. Everyone did. When you set aside whatever your political differences and agendas might be, you find out that there are no big differences in all kinds of animals. They like sports, they like to eat, they love their farm, and in the case of Pete and Rex, surprise, they liked women. Pete also liked how Rex ruled the farm. Once after a midterm where Rex's administration lost a lot of seats thanks to the efforts of a hardline member of the Elephant party, a newt named Grinch who had a manifesto contract for the

Rainbow Farm, Rex adjusted. Rex was savvy enough to read the tea leaves and move back to the center, which was the opposite of what Cam had done when faced with the same situation. Cam refused to move at all digging in on his current position and treating the voters like their votes did not matter. Pete always admired that flexibility in Rex and decided at some point in the conversation, he would ask Rex about that move.

Pete said, "Wow, Rex, you digressed, tell me more about this eagle."

"Yes, I do that at times. Usually, it is a young hen that sidetracks me." He said this with a chuckle. "So yes, I noticed this eagle following me one day, and it said nothing the first time, but after he figured out who I was, he started doing it every time I was out on a walkabout. One day, he seemed to be singing, and as he got closer, I was able to discern some lyrics: 'Kick 'em when they're up, kick 'em when they're down.' What on earth is going on here? I thought to myself.

"Finally, I said, 'Hey, eagle, come on down here and let's talk.'"

"What a strange sight that must have been—an eagle and a rooster having a discussion in the middle of a pasture."

"'What's your name, eagle?' I asked.

"'Donnie,' he said.

"'I'm Rex,' I said.

"'I know who you are, everyone does,' said Donnie.

"'Why are you following me, Donnie?'

"'Well, Rex,' he says, 'One day, I was flying around with my friend Glenn, and Glenn said to me, Isn't it amazing how our songs seem to apply to all walks of life but lately I can't help but to think of Rex when I sing our lyrics? After that, when Glenn and I would fly around, we would sing our songs and both of us would look for things we thought applied to you."

"'That's fascinating,' I said to Donnie. 'Curiosity is killing me. Can you share some of those?'

"'Sure,' says Donnie. 'I would love to do that. I so much enjoyed soaring with Glenn, and sharing these stories helps keep his memories alive for me.'"

Pete said, "Wow, Rex, that is quite a story. I'm curious as well. What were the songs and lyrics he shared?"

Rex said, "You should be, because what he told me applies to everyone and especially you with the pedestal you may eventually hold, if you beat Shrill," he said with a laugh.

"So the first set of lyrics—kick 'em when they're up, kick 'em when they're down—Donnie says those words are a true reflection of the gotcha society we live in. How the public fueled by the media fixates on dirty laundry."

"I agree," said Rex. "It was dirty laundry, especially a blue dress with a stain that brought me down."

"'Yeah,' chimed in Donnie, 'and it was a bubble-headed bleached blonde that went after me.'

"'What else?' I asked Donnie.

"'Well, Rex,' he said, 'sometimes you seem like a Desperado, trying to come to your senses, out riding fences, and for you, the things that are pleasing you can hurt you somehow."

"'Wow,' I thought," said Rex. 'Nothing could be truer. The things I have always loved have been my downfall—food, women, all coming back to haunt me.'

"Donnie continued, 'I and Glenn used to notice you spent a lot of time in the Hen House. Well, we know you are not an avid egg collector so we assume you had other business there, and it always seemed to be late at night, therefore…late at night, a big old barn gets lonely. I guess every form of refuge has its price, and it breaks his heart to think his love is only given to a woman with claws as cold as ice and throws things at him. I might add,' with a laugh. 'You had those lying eyes, Pete.'"

Rex said to Pete, "I took this in not as an indictment but the truth. I did do those things, and I wasn't proud of them and was not trying to hurt anyone in the process, but I felt in my heart that I could walk and chew gum at the same time. I could cheat on my wife, right or wrong, and at the same time still faithfully execute the office of Chief of the Rainbow Farm. I never have understood why the other side was trying to hang me on this matter, and the hypocrisy of it all really hit home. These are animals that profess to be accepting and forgiving but they seemed to only adhere to their teachings when it suited them. Where was the practice of judge not, and you shall not be judged. Why were they all throwing stones from their respective glass houses?"

"Do you know there is a special slush fund set aside on the farm that is used to settle out of court any time a male or female accuses our leaders of sexual harassment? They silence them with money, it's a standard practice. And on this list are Donkeys and Elephants. I say make it transparent. I would love to have this list during a State of the Farm speech and expose those hucksters."

"So let me finish how my conversation with Donnie went. I then said to Donnie, 'Let him who is without sin cast the first stone. According to the Gospel of John, the Pharisees, to discredit Jesus, brought a woman charged with adultery before him. Jesus thought for a moment and then replied, "He that is without sin among you, let him cast the first stone at her." For me, it seemed that in my situation, no one listened to Jesus and so many were throwing rocks that we no longer had to contract having land cleared on the farm for growing crops."

"'Well, Rex,' said Donnie, 'it comes with the territory. Seems to me there is so much character assassination these days that no one wants to run for office. It is a blood sport on the farm and attacking individuals and their families shortens the list of those who want to serve because they do not want their family name and loved ones dragged through the muck in the process of running. And I hate to inform you, Rex, you have now checked into the White Barn and you can never leave. It truly is your heaven and your hell.'

Rex said to Pete, "I grew to love their music more and more, such meaning and such truth. No doubt in my opinion the greatest group of singers and storytellers ever to grace us with their presence here on Rainbow Farm."

Pete was fascinated by what Rex was telling him. All politics aside, Rex was a male, an animal that just happened to be a politician and held the highest office in the land. Holding this office never changed the fact that Pete was an animal doing animal things and subject to the same temptations all animals from all walks of life were exposed to. He also sympathized with Rex and how he was attacked for the most trivial of matters. He was experiencing some of this already. Rex being an animal from the south was made fun of for how he talked. "He can't be intelligent if he talks slow with an accent," they would say. The same was being done to him for his accent from the Big Apple where he grew up. How ridiculous, he thought, that people would judge him for how he spoke, and these were the same ones preaching diversity. Hypocrisy just kept reentering the conversation.

Pete said, "Rex, I do really appreciate you sharing this insight with me. I must admit it makes me wonder if I am doing the right thing in running for this office. Is it worth it and can I make a difference?"

Rex said, "Looking back I ask myself if the juice was worth the squeeze and I will be very truthful and say yes it was. All of the character assassination, some true, a lot not, seems everything was a gate, gate this, and gate that, file gate, travel gate, Yellow Farm gate. Like the stone throwers, these clowns assigned a gate moniker every time I farted, breathed, no matter what I did. If it kept up, we would be a farm with lots of gates and no rocks. Pete, no matter what you do, it will be criticized. You could walk on water and they will say see, I told you he could not swim. You could cure cancer and they would say you were putting doctors out of business. You could give everyone a million dollars, and they would swear you could have given a million plus one that you were just too cheap to part with that extra dollar. Despite all that, the good that you can bring to the lives of all the farm animals squares the equation. It's all worth it. Meeting all the animals on the farm regardless of their economic standing or positions has made me a better animal. I feel fulfilled by this experience and would not trade it for anything."

Pete thought to himself, *This guy is brilliant. I wish I had him in my camp. I can't believe that Shrill and Little Tookie don't listen to his advice. This is great news for me. If Shrill and her sycophants and merry little band of yes men and women were not smart enough to listen to Rex, then maybe, just maybe, he, Pete, had a chance to win this thing.*

PETE: I am curious, Rex—when several Donkeys lost that midterm, you decided to, in a political sense, move to the center. Can you tell me why?

REX: Sure, Pete. Most animals on the farm are actually more alike than different. They, regardless if from the party of Elephants or Donkeys, are either center-left CL or center-right CR in the political spectrum. Dead center between CL and CR are your independents who are prone to swinging to either elephants or donkeys in general elections. I call them the Swingers. And I know a few things about Swingers, no pun intended [*he laughs*]. Win them Swingers, and you win the White Barn. As you move further left or right from the center, you will experience fringe elements. Neither side have a monopoly on whackos, but the kooks are such a minority they are not worth even soliciting. It's the Swingers, Pete, the Swingers!

PETE: Why did Cam not do the same thing when he lost midterm seats?

REX: Pure arrogance. And one of the downfalls of his character—and I would argue Shrill has this problem as well. Entrenching yourself and refusing to adjust your policies based on the barometer that these midterms provide is just, well, plain stupid. In effect, the animals are providing you an azimuth check and what type of rudder steer you as the captain of the ship need to make to satisfy the animals. You don't ignore this—it becomes a critical part of your calculus and how you keep people in your tent. How you expand the tent, how you stay on top. To disregard results of a midterm is a mistake.

If Rex had looked in a crystal ball at that moment, he would have seen Pete making the same mistake. If analyzing the three, Rex, Cam, and Pete, you would see that Rex separated himself from both Cam and Pete about how each reacted to these midterms. Rex was the one with the vision, political savviness, and smart enough to move with the flow. Cam and Pete were both arrogant and stubborn enough to the point of not moving at all. That would cost both politically.

The night was winding down and the two men exchanged pleasant goodbyes.

PETE: Rex, I really appreciate you taking the time to talk with me this evening. What you have told me has been very inspiring and helpful to me not as a candidate, which I am sure were not your intentions, but as a man. You took the time and treated me as a fellow animal. A fellow male, a comrade, dare I say a friend.

REX: No worries, Pete, I wish you the best. I hope you come in second, but if you win, you will be my Chief, but more importantly, the Chief of all the animals. Godspeed, Pete. See you on the trail, and as a favor, we never saw each other tonight. Try to keep it on the down low.

As Pete was walking back home, he reflected on the conversation. While walking, he ran into an old friend from the Big Apple, a Doberman pincher named G-man, a former mayor and lawyer. "Pete, where have you been? You look deep in thought."

"You would not believe it if you had been there yourself, I just spent hours talking with Rex," replied Pete.

"Are you kidding me?" said G-man. "I would not spend five minutes with that knucklehead. You can't be serious, Pete. I thought you didn't drink. See you around."

That brief encounter with G-man was icing on the cake. Everything Rex had told him was validated by G-man's comments. It really was a bloodthirsty arena he was about to enter. You were either on one side or the other. Compromise would be next to impossible. Pete had visions in his head, and they were not pleasant. He was about to enter an arena where it would be a zero sum result. For there to be a winner, there would have to be a loser. Heck in some instances with the system of the Eggtorial College the losing candidate could win a plurality of the popular vote and still lose the general election.

How would he rule in such an environment? Would not gridlock be the norm? How could you please one side without offending the other? No matter what he did it would end up making the other side angry. They would attack him and his family. He could take it, but he did have concerns for his wife, who being from another farm had no idea what she was signing up for. How would she handle such attacks? Pete decided then and there he would not take anything lying down. If they came after him, he would counterpunch with a vengeance. He would not heed to scripture where in the good book it read, "Do not take *revenge*, my dear friends, but leave room for God's wrath, for it is written, 'It is *mine* to avenge. I will repay,' says the Lord.

Pete would not wait on the Lord to repay; he would deal with them himself. And the lower they dared to go, he would go with them. He wasn't afraid of getting dirty. Before speaking with Rex, he did not really believe he had a chance of winning, and to be honest, there was a little bit of truth that all of this was some sort of publicity stunt because his entire life he had been in the spotlight and revealed in publicity. But after this candid conversation with Rex, he learned a lot about Rex but even more about himself. Rex changed Pete that night. How ironic that the husband of his opponent would be what changed Pete for the better. He came away with an entirely different view and even more resolve to win.

The Campaign Comes to a Close, Election Night

CHIEF OF FARM DEBATES

Shrill and Pete would face off in three debates that were being labeled as "The Battle of the Birds." Every animal on the farm to include those who wanted Pete to win expected Shrill to chew Pete up and spit him out like an unwanted hairball. After all, this was her world, her arena, and she was not about to let some two-bit peacock come in and beat her at her game. But Pete did surprisingly well, and it was his quick wit that would come across as the highlight of all three debates. Ever the counterpuncher, it was Pete who when degraded by Shrill's comment, "It is a good thing that someone with the temperament of Pete is not in charge of the farm." fired back with, "Because you would be locked in a bird cage."

As Pete was prone to do, he gave Shrill a nickname. "Shrill, you are now known as Sideways Shrill. Why, because you have never flown a straight line in your life."

That really made Shrill angry, and she retorted, "Well, Pete, when will you show us your tax returns?"

"When you give Marcellus his hammer back," chuckled Pete.

Pete was also one step ahead of Shrill and her team, knowing when she found the opportunity, she would attack Pete, labeling him as misogynist. Pete invited four old hens who all had previously accused Rex of sexual harassment and sat them on the front row. It worked; Shrill never came after him on that front. During one of the debates Pete went into peacock strut mode and while Shrill was answering a question from the moderator kept walking behind her. Shrill would later cry, "He is creepy. He made my tail feathers stand up." So these debates ended, and if one were to analyze them collectively, they might conclude that Pete won. Not because he out-did Shrill but for the fact he was still standing. As for Shrill, she underperformed because she failed to deliver the knockout blow that would have sent Pete's supporters to the exit and would in effect turn the last month of her campaign into a glorified mop up operation. That did not happen.

The debates were over, and what seemed like an eternity leading up to the day of all days was over and Election Day was here. Almost everyone did not give Pete a chance to win. To be honest, even he did not think he had a chance, but beyond everyone's wildest dreams, no one ever thought he would make it this far. A peacock, flash in the pan, neophyte, non-politician, businessman, cad, bigot—what chance did he have of winning Chief of the Farm? It would never happen. The bearded stork, Rad, Pete's numbers guy, thought differently. As an animal known for his ability to read data and numbers, he ensured his boss Pete that he was going to win. "Well, Pete's stork may be brilliant with analyzing data and numbers, but Shrill has this in the bag," was the consensus among all Donkeys and many Elephants.

ELECTION NIGHT

Shrill, Rex, her campaign manager, Tookie, a chipmunk, and head advisor, Po, a polecat, had gathered on election night for what was to be her coronation. Although she had run a terrible campaign by alienating certain parts of the farm either by outright insult (gonna put the moles out of business, deplorables) or not even visiting them (Dairy Belt), she was still arrogant to the point that she felt she had it in the bag. Her young campaign manager, Tookie, was also super confident, as well as Po. Rex, however, did not share the same level of confidence. He felt that Shrill's spending most of the time in her comfort zone and in echo chambers had given her a false sense of security. All the major networks had Shrill leading in the polls and easily winning this. Thus, it was a matter of time for the ceiling to be shattered and for the Shrill Coronation. A first was about to occur. A female parrot would be Chief of the Rainbow Farm.

Early coverage had Rex and Shrill in a giggly mood like two high school kids on prom night as they jumped out to an early lead. Embassies on other farms invited the entire diplomatic international community to their workplace to witness what was to be history. At the invite of ambassadors, they had gathered to see firsthand how democracy should work. At one event, the local staff had been solicited to help blow up balloons to be released once it was determined Shrill had won the election. But the glass was never to be shattered, and the balloons would never fall (later an investigation was launched into why Rainbow tax payer dollars were used for local workers to blow up balloons for a victory celebration for just one of the candidates. Like every other investigation dealing with Teflon Rex and Shrill it seemed to go nowhere).

The irony of all this was that all the other farm representatives from around the world gathered at the Rainbow Embassy on Red Farm and would be first hand witnesses to a thing of beauty; a fair and democratic election that would eventually be seen by many as unfair and illegitimate. Elections are zero sum games; someone wins, so someone must lose. What is the most critical aspect of the process is the fairness and legality of the voting. Who votes, who can vote, and how the vote is counted. There are two ways to look at this. If the result is that the heavily favored candidate did not win, then the result was completely legitimate as many of the invited observers from other farms exclaimed, "Wow, democracy must work on your farm. This would never happen on our farm where the favorite with the backing of the establishment would lose." The counterpoint would be that the underdog must have rigged the election. That might be possible if the underdog was part of the establishment with the benefit of support from the current administration and his bully pulpit, but that wasn't the case here. Pete did not have the backing and support of the political machine of the farm, but he tapped into something more important than that support. He connected with the animals. At the end of the day, support is not a metric, votes are, and Pete got the votes he needed, especially those from the Swing Belts that would propel him to victory.

There actually was a first that night. A candidate with no military or political experience was elected as Chief of the Farm. At first it had looked bleak for Pete. Early returns and exit polls showed him behind and projected to lose. But then something happened. Pete, who knew that he would never win the hen house, the Apple gang, or Beavers, started racking up victories across the board in places he knew all along as his best chance to amass the total needed to win. The Gators who were large in number went his way. The Wolverines in a squeaker landed in his column. The white-tailed deer of Buckeye land was another major victory. But the kicker was Pete pulling in the Dairy Belt, his draw to his inside straight. When the Dairy Cows fell into Pete's win column, suddenly it was Shrill that was drawing to an inside straight and having the narrow path to victory. It was a long shot; she desperately needed a 2 for her Ace, 3, 4, 5. One small problem, Pete had all the deuces.

If the balloons would have been released that early morning just past midnight, they would have fallen straight to the ground. Like the personalities across the land that had gone all in for Shrill they were severely deflated. Inside the convention hall where all the Donkeys had gathered for a victory ceremony it was quite as a mouse. All the talking heads on the Shrill News Network, SNN, looked as if someone had rained on their parade or they were attending a funeral. Suddenly it happened—the election was called, and the ceiling parted, but no balloons fell. Instead, it was a huge Sour Grape Asteroid that once it hit shattered into thousands of miniature sour grapes quickly consumed by the huddled masses as they stood around in a physical state of despair. Some cried, some remained stoic, the Beavers hung their heads, and the once loud boisterous clucks of the hens became weak, wimbly clucks. One red-faced hen gave the "up yours" signal, which is a claw raised in the air with the middle appendage extended in exaggerated fashion.

"What a spectacle!" exclaimed a Pete supporter. "Go home. Get some rest. All will be well. The republic will still be here in the morning."

A new name for the fickle was born that night, Dandelions. In the farmyard, dandelions spring up all over, but whenever a strong wind comes up, they seem to disappear. The hall was full of Dandelions. Young and old animals alike were crying like babies that night just because their candidate had lost. Sly, a conniving fox and leader of the Red Farm, along with his cronies across the land howled with laughter at this spectacle. Sly chuckled, "Is this the gene pool they plan to recruit for future armies? May their God help them."

As the sour grapes began to be digested by the Dandelions, the complaints and excuses came pouring out.

"How could Pete win?" clucked an old hen. "Every hen I know voted for Shrill."

Another kangaroo from the Fruit Belt and employed as an Apple gatherer said something similar.

The Beavers said the same. "All Beavers voted for Shrill—how can this be? The Eggtorial College sucks, rotten eggs they are, why are the cows in Dairyland getting more votes than we are?" And on and on it went.

Over in Pete's area of operations, it was completely different. They had done it, pulling off the biggest upset ever seen in an election for Chief of the Farm. Whose turn was it to laugh now? "Give me a phone," said Pete. "I wanna call Cam first and tell him to pick up that mic he dropped when he said to me, 'Well, Pete, at least I am

Chief of the Farm.' Then I will call Shrill and pass my thanks from all the deplorables who voted for us and especially the moles she wanted to put out of business. Oh, happy day!"

Back at the Shrill HQ, all had gone quiet. Shrill was nowhere to be seen, and later accounts had her in the fetal position in her hotel room. Everyone kept their distance. Rex tried to approach and console her, but she threw a hammer at him. "Where did the hammer come from?" cried Rex. "An ashtray is bad enough, but a hammer?" Must have been Shrill's hammer because it had *MINE* stenciled on the handle.

Shrill would not be seen that early morning after the election was called. It took a call from Cam to basically order her to concede the election. Before conceding the election, she could not even face her supporters. Poor Po had to come out and face the music for her. "It's been a long night. Keep the faith. There's still hope. Go home and lay your wee little heads down on your wee little pillows, and all will be okay." Later, Po would muse he felt like Pinocchio and could feel his nose literally growing as he spoke. I guess straight talk was out of the question.

CHAPTER SIX

The Aftermath

So begin the autopsy. How did Shrill lose and even more startling how did Pete win? Instead of embracing and accepting what the foreigners had witnessed, democracy at its best, the losing side would show democracy at its worst. Was there an outside influence? Why not learn from your mistakes and get ready for the next general election? That did not happen, and what would begin would be a never-ending saga of finger pointing, baseless accusations, cashing in Nova's insurance policy, and an outright coup to overturn the results of the election and get Pete out and Shrill in. In conjunction would be the syntax dance of word play.

"You spied," said the Elephants.

"No, we didn't. We just surveilled and investigated," countered the Donkeys.

"Your top cops under Cam were involved in staging a coup," the Elephants cried.

"No, we were attempting an illegal seizure of the government," laughed the Donkeys.

And finally, in desperation just to make a point, "You are breathing air through your lungs, aren't you?" said the Elephants, finally thinking they had backed the Donkeys into a corner.

"No, actually, we are pulling air into our lungs, and technically, not all of us have lungs. Some have gills. Don't forget the fish," the Donkeys snickered and brayed.

"Dang!" the elephants muttered to themselves. "These dang donkeys give new meaning to the term *smart ass*."

Was there an outside influence? Many believed that the Red Farm was responsible for Shrill losing the election. They even went further, accusing Pete of colluding and cooperating with the Red Farm to defeat Shrill. So what was it with Pete? Was he the bumbling idiot who talked funny and was the Donkey's proclaimed Idiot-in-Chief, or was he this Machiavellian genius able to conspire with a foreign farm and take down an opponent who went into the general election ahead by twenty points? Which one was he? He couldn't be both. Would the real Pete please stand up? Besides, it was Cam himself who declared leading up to the election in response to something Pete said about accepting election results, "Sly and the Red Farm cannot influence our election. Our system is too decentralized. I advise Pete to quit whining and go out and campaign and get more votes." So again, you cannot have it both ways. Either Cam was clueless and had got it completely wrong on the Red Farm's ability to influence an election or he was correct (which he was) and now the Donkey's once again had changed the truth, exercised selective memory, and concocted a narrative to account for Shrill's loss. It just could not be something as simple as Shrill ran a bad campaign, failed to listen to Rex, and lost. Surely not. This wasn't over and, like a ticking time bomb, was soon to explode once Pete officially entered office. In the meantime, Cam's administration had some 'splaining to do and some serious reverse engineering to cover their tracks.

Time for the insurance policy. If Shrill would have won, one wonders if the Red Farm collusion story would have ever made it out of the womb. A betting animal says no. The second and third order effects of Pete winning was exposure of the deep state and nasty political underbelly of the Rainbow Farm. One can just see the Toad, Orangutan, and Giraffe election night. As it became more and more evident that Pete would win and that they had all hedged their bets on Shrill winning, they realized they were in serious T-R-O-U-B-L-E. Imagine them at the roulette table. "Oh, heaven help us," grunted the Toad. "We have placed all our chips on *red*."

"You idiots!" screamed the Orangutan. "You told me we had this in the bag." Even AC, who normally was smart enough to thread the needle and go 50/50 RED and BLACK this time had also gone all RED. They were not only collectively in trouble—they were S-C-R-E-W-E-D. So they either took it in the shorts or they double-downed. Out came the shovels, and they commenced to trying to dig from the hole they found themselves.

Poor Shrill. "They were never going to let me be president." Begs the question, who is they? Seems she, the Donkeys, and the media provided the answer. Of course, it was the Red Farm and Sly and Pete colluding to take her down. Nothing to do with not taking the advice of Rex to campaign outside her comfort zone. Heaven forbid it was simply a case of her being a bad candidate exacerbated by the fact she got it all wrong on the trail. It had to be something else. The day after, she and Rex took a long walk in the forest with a jug of the farm's best Jungle Juice in tow. That would become her signature response to all questions from her beloved followers as she slowly came out of hiding and faced the music. "How are you doing, Shrill? How are you holding up?" asked her groupies.

"Just fine," replied Shrill. "Long walks in the forest and lots of Jungle Juice are my self-medication."

One Elephant countered with, "Thank Goodness she didn't win, can you see the Situation Room in a world crisis when the going got tough?"

"Where's Shrill? We need a decision," the staff would cry.

"Oh, she got rattled, and last I saw, she was headed into the forest with a walking stick and a jug of Jungle Juice," would be the reply.

The Hen's March

So the countdown began, and tomorrow would be the big day when Pete would be sworn in and officially become the Chief of the Rainbow Farm. But it would be a day unlike any other as the opposition was about to shift into high gear. Something was going on in the hen house—what was it? Seems they were up to something. Egg production was down. Even Rex was turned away at the door as they were too busy for shenanigans, and they had a real mission and operation in the works. On the day after Pete's inauguration, their operation kicked into high gear. The Hens' March would be the largest protest ever on the farm. Oh, how the hens clucked. They had gathered in front of the White Barn to voice their displeasure with Pete taking office. *Cluck, cluck, cluck* filled the air as they marched in protest. One of the strangest types of headwear ever to be seen on the farm made its debut that day. At first glance, one had to do a double take but after a second these hens all had pink hats on that resembled the exact location on a female hen where eggs were dispatched. Said the baby chick to his mother, "Mama, what kind of hat is that?"

What to say? Either say it was what it was or hide behind symbolism. Mama choose the latter. "That is an anti-Pete hat, and it stands for our solidarity." The fact that hens would bring baby chicks to an event wearing these hats and their vulgar language spoke volumes to their character, not Pete's.

The maintenance man Marcellus viewing from afar just muttered to himself, "The madness continues. Oh, what tangled webs we weave. Where the heck is my hammer?"

Some of the more well-known hens got up to make speeches. They mostly attacked Pete's physical characteristics, but one old bird known for her chops back in the day threatened to blow up the White Barn. Another disgruntled, washed-up hen clucked, "I'm not as nasty as a peacock who looks like he bathes in pumpkin juice, who is a ridiculous concoction of feathers and whose words are a distraction to the Rainbow Farm. He spews Eggtorial College-sanctioned hate speech contaminating our beloved Rainbow Farm anthem." This would become the so-called Nasty Speech and the Hen's rallying cry. One had to wonder how Pete could muster up so much hate, and he had not even been in office twenty-four hours. What an event, the most ridiculous spectacle ever seen on the farm to date.

"*Cluck, cluck, cluck,* Pete must go."

"*Cluck, cluck, cluck,* we hate Pete."

"*Cluck, cluck, cluck,* Pete is a misogynist."

"*Cluck, cluck, cluck,* the Eggtorial College is full of rotten eggs."

There was no honeymoon for Pete as normally afforded to new Chiefs and, in effect, no quarter. Day one and the resistance was off with a bang, or cluck. In fact, lots of clucks.

I'm not nasty like a peacock

The Crows

"Dang crows." The Chief of Interior Farm Security, CIFS, was talking to himself. "It's bad enough they steal from the cash crops on the farm, but the latest is them flying all over the farm, making all kinds of false accusations and attacking the boss man. I thought the clucking hens were bad, but this is ridiculous." The crows he was referring two were two older female crows who constantly flew around the farm cawing away such phrases as "Impeach Pete!" These two old birds, Max and Leila, were conspicuous for the way they chose to protect their heads from the sun. Due to thinning hair on top, one wore a cowboy hat, and the other a ridiculous-looking wig.

In one episode of their rebel rousing, it was Max who cawed, "Attack Pete's supporters, go to where they eat, where they congregate, wherever they are and harass them. Confront them at the troughs, the well *caw, caw, caw!*"

TWEETER

Pete was smart enough to realize that the main stream press and media were Anti-Pete. They had been that way to him as a businessman; they had continued that approach throughout his campaign and he knew it would continue through his time in office. They hated him then, and they hated him even more now that he had won. He decided that he would by pass them in getting his message out to the common animals on the farm. He refused the press and media the opportunity to filter and spin his message. He had a special dislike for the rags *Farmyard Gazette* and *Hitching Post*. So he decided to heck with talking through organizations—he would go straight talk to the people. He organized a group of loyal yellow canaries and used a system known as Tweeter. Every day, sometimes on the hour, he would employ a posse of these cute little birds and send them out with his message of the day or hour.

On one particular incident, it was Max who when delivering one of her inspiring messages to her masses got flustered because in the background listening to her speech was a small inconspicuous yellow canary working for Pete and annotating everything Max said. "I know what you little yellow birds are up to," cried Max and began flying after the small bird, but she was too old and slow and the yellow canary, nicknamed Speedy, flew back to Pete. He was then quickly loaded up with a counter narrative, and off flew Speedy and his friends to deliver the real-time response from Pete. How he loved his Tweeter. Here was Pete's Tweeter response to the Hens' March: "Angry females call me names, foul language in front of puppies, calves, and kittens, all hypocrites, MFGA…"

Say hello to my little yellow friends

CHAPTER SEVEN

The Coup

A perfect day of diversion from the Hens' March was an opportunity to cash in the insurance policy. Inside a hidden house which Rex kept for his trysts, a different type of meeting was taking place. Gathered around the table were AC the Giraffe, Rex the Rooster, Ed the Toad, Caesar the Orangutan, Fancy the Bat, Crier the Cat, Naddie the Walrus, Shifty the Weasel, Nova the Bluebird, Stein the Opossum, and of all things, an unknown snake from the Limey Farm. Although not seen, you could feel the presence of Cam. Apparently, he had gone into fly on the wall mode and was invisible. You knew he was there; you just couldn't see him. In the back of the room, looking like she had been crying since election night, was Shrill. The Giraffe, although junior in rank, opened the meeting.

AC: I am calling to order this meeting to kick off Operation Takedown Pete. Shrill, you have the floor.

SHRILL: Well, AC, are you with me or against me? By your actions just before the election, which were one of the reasons I lost, I'm not sure I need or want your support. I hope you have a plan that supports me instead of kills me. You are wishy-washy. Which side of the fence are you on today?

AC: Okay, Shrill, I admit that may have hurt you, but I, like everyone else, was sure you had it in the bag. We didn't think you would blow it and lose. Furthermore, a big part of that loss wasn't me—it was your pathetic campaign.

CAESAR: Okay, let's stay on message. Nothing will change the results of the election night. We need to address the mission at hand, Takedown Pete, Operation TP. Ed and Nova, any ideas? Nova, what was this insurance policy you spoke of with Mona?

Shrill went back to her cage and commenced to hitting the jug. Fancy looked over, wishing she could join.

NOVA: Our insurance policy was planned in the event we had a catastrophic event defined simply as Pete winning.

ED: We know the Red Farm interfered in our election. Is there a way to show that Pete or his campaign or his staff cooperated with or colluded with the Red Farm in their activities? Make it appear that Pete was in collusion with Sly to steal the election from Shrill?

NOVA: I had a tail on Pete one night when he was eating at the diner. He used Red Farm Salad Dressing.

Oh, my, thought Rex. *I wonder if they tailed him the night we had our long talk.*

ED: That's it, Red Farm Salad Dressing. He must be colluding with the Red Farm.

NADDIE: I agree. I bet he didn't pay for that dressing with his own money. Perhaps we get him on the emolument's clause. I would bet he even has stocks for Red Farm Salad Dressing in his portfolio. We must subpoena all his financial records. Where's Max?

NOVA: Good idea, Nads, I think we come at him from several different angles. We high-low him from all directions, we go after him for anything regardless if warranted, regardless if legitimate, all out attrition warfare, his family, and anyone associated with him. We will pluck one feather at a time until he is fully exposed for all his transgressions, actual and concocted.

AC: Nova, can you go into detail on the plan?

NOVA: Well, many of you are wondering who this Limey is at the meeting. His name is Snake because he is a snake and does snake like things. Snake is a much-respected professional spy from our sister division from the Limey Farm. Snake you have the floor—er, perhaps you should speak from the table.

SNAKE: I have a piece of paper here that is a report that is information I got from the Red Farm that proves Pete was cooperating with the Red Farm to take down Shrill.

CAESAR: Can you verify these sources?

SNAKE: No, but that is not important, I can assure you everything is true. Just ask Sir Andy Log he will vouch for me. I will feed this report to someone in Pete's own party, a never Peter, we will refer to him as NP.

AC: Once I get word you have fed NP, I will request a meeting with him, and when he provides me the report, that will be the basis of our investigation. We can also use this report to surveil those associated with Pete.

ED: I know a judge who will accept this at face value and give us what we want to legally spy—er, I mean surveil on Pete's associates.

AC: I know Pete hates me—jealous of my big hooves, and stature, I might add [*he chuckles*]. I will get him to fire me. I want no part of his administration anyway. Once I do that, we will up the ante and somehow initiate a special council for Pete firing me over opening an investigation on something that didn't happen. This is beautiful. Anyone with connections on how to get the council going?

CAESAR: Too easy. I will notify the current Top Cop that we have evidence of him cooperating with the Red Farm. Even though it was not cooperation and not different in any way, shape, or form from what previous administrations did in reaching out during a transition, he will fall for the ruse and recuse himself from the entire affair and be powerless to counter our efforts or help Pete in any way. That's where you come in, Stieny. As deputy to the Top Cop, you can then convene a special counsel to investigate Pete's cooperation with the Red Farm, and as we all know, Pete once hit with this, will retaliate, counterpunch—it's his nature, like the scorpion who stings the frog, a Red Farm parable, how ironic [*snickers*]. Once he counterpunches, and he will, we then go after him for obstruction for investigation into a crime he did not commit in the first place.

The entire room erupted into laughter, the snake hissed, the walrus waddled and barked, Shrill did a slurry chirp, Shifty was break dancing on the table, Fancy flapped her wings vigorously and flew around the room, finally bumping into an invisible Cam. She then fell landing next to Shrill. "Can I have a swig?" she said to Shrill. The Crier cried but with joy. Caesar pounded his chest and howled. AC stood tall, towering above the room, his head leaned back obviously in a state of ecstasy, proud of his efforts in what he perceived as saving the Rainbow Farm.

The only silent one in this was Rex. He wanted no part of this. He felt it was unfair to take such action. He himself had been on the receiving end of such nonsense, and he knew there was no upside to this partisan witch-hunt. It was bad not for just those involved but had significant second- and third-order effects that would affect innocent people. He wished he never knew about this.

NADDIE: This is a brilliant strategy. I envision a Constitutional crisis on the horizon, all because of Pete, that sidewinder.

FANCY: I will remain neutral to sell a semblance of fairness, resist calls for impeachment. Crier, you should go around doing what you do best, cry about all things unfair. Paint Pete as a bad guy.

CRIER: I know I cry a lot but how can I keep it up?
AC: We have a special super-duper cry machine. You conceal
            cut onions under your vest, and a special button releases
            those fumes to your eyes—voila, instant crying.
SHIFTY: I will be all over the farm, misleading the dumb animals.
            Ensuring them I got the goods on Pete and that it will all
            come out in the report.

So the meeting winded down. The animals could not believe that they had hatched such a brilliant scheme, Operation TP, had a nice ring to it.

Finally, it was Caesar the Orangutan who made a statement followed by a question.

CAESAR: Colleagues this is a brilliant plan, however when ana-
            lyzing it the most critical keystone to this operation will
            be who is assigned to lead the investigation and special
            council against Pete. Anybody know a good candidate?
AC: That's easy, Devil Dog.

Yeah, we got this, Pete's going down

Cam, high on a beam and out of sight, just sat there and smiled.

Looking back the plan, the cabal hatched that day was simple. Everyone agreed that the Red Farm was bad. It did not matter that Cam had reached out to them through Shrill proposing that a reset policy with the Red farm was a good thing. Was it not the same Red Farm referred to in a debate from the last election when Cam's opponent declared the Red Farm as a threat and Cam had replied, "The eighties called, they want their foreign policy back," begs the question what was so different now? Easy answer, Pete. Pete, who used to be loved by the asses and donated money to their campaigns. Pete a former ass himself, (no pun intended). But Pete, much like the oligarchs on the Red Farm, was a businessman who made the horrible transgression of entering the political arena and threatening the establishment to include Donkeys as well as many Elephants.

There is a saying that power corrupts and absolute power corrupts absolutely. No one could ever had predicted .that these gentlemen who had served so honorably over the years could do any wrong. Could they? Time would tell, but bottom line, it seemed Pete somehow had become a very powerful enemy of the state. Why, who knows, but there were several theories: jealousy, sour grapes for beating Shrill, but most of all, arrogance. These well-educated animals knew better than a bunch of deplorables who clung to their guns, Bible, God, and religion what was best for the farm. They would make things right. It was their calling, and whether the intentions were benevolent, driven by standard operating practice and modus operandi, saving the ship, their actions were misguided at best and borderline seditious. It remained to be seen how all this would play out.

One serious miscalculation they made was they assumed incorrectly that once they went after Pete, he would basically be isolated and pretty much on his own. The fact he had received slightly less popular votes than Shrill did not register into their calculus. That this portion of the electorate would sit idly by and let Pete be taken down seemed to escape their planning. Although most of the press was Anti-Pete, there were bastions of conservative press that would vigorously defend Pete. But not all the Elephants would defend Pete.

Many from a group of rhinos were Never Peters. Many from the Elephant party were scared to be identified as staunch Pete supporters in the event the preposterous charges from the Donkeys were true. But not all. Many with powerful standing and large microphones vigorously defended Pete from the very beginning, and as it became more and more apparent that the investigation into Pete was bogus the momentum shifted and what initially was a hasty defense matured over time into a strong point, complete with its own improved parapets, counterattack weaponry, and information operations that would expose the cabal and its efforts.

THE COFFEE PARTY

One group of Wolverines in the Elephant party that met for coffee weekly were square in the corner of Pete. Unlike some of their colleagues, especially the rhinoceroses, these tough-as-nail individuals stuck behind Pete through thick and thin. They were always very sharply dressed in coat and tie, except for a shorter one named Jimmie. He was a "roll up your sleeves" kind of guy and tough as nails. He was especially known for his wrestling skills and tenacity and the one you wanted in your corner. If it was the truth you were looking for, then Jimmie was your man. Time and time again, the Wolverines would defend Pete based on what they knew was an attempt to falsely accuse a duly elected Chief of Farm. It was the type of group you either love or hated, depending of course if one was an Ass or Elephant.

CHAPTER EIGHT

One and the Same

Rainbow and Red Farms

When one compares the Red Farm and Rainbow Farm and how these two distinctly different farms with different histories handled their political opponents it becomes apparent their objectives were the same. Like most in power, they wanted no outsiders. How they went about doing this, their modus operandi was different. Sly used a much more proactive approach. He simply threw his competition in jail before they got on the ballot. It was cheaper, direct, and set precedence and additionally sent a chilling message to all businessman who fancied themselves a politician and dared enter the political arena. After all, they had been warned to stay in their respective lanes and could have all the perks they wanted if—and a big if—they did not cross the line. The Rainbow Farm conversely used a reactive approach. They were so cocksure that Shrill would win and that the unthinkable of Pete winning would never happen.

So while Sly's competition was rotting away in a pen, the Donkey's opponent had pulled off the impossible and was now CoF. The Donkeys then conspired and went after a duly elected official, who was now in an advantageous position of strength able to effectively counter their shenanigans. So again, comparing again to how Sly went about it and how the Donkeys did it, consider this—Sly spent nothing, no hours spent unnecessarily on ridiculous investigations and no exhaustive amount of resource. The Donkeys, on the other hand, went the opposite direction. A select few waited until after the fact when a candidate they despised had won an election and then conspired to overthrow that candidate resulting in millions of resources spent on a bogus investigation. This resulted in complete gridlock and precious time wasted off the legislative calendar, which should have been used to conduct the business of the farm's animals.

If you look at Sly's means strictly from a pragmatic view, one could argue he got it right regarding efficiency, cost, and no second- and third-order effects. One who opposed Sly's method might say it was unethical and ignored the rule of law. The counter to that might be was how a cabal and an unfounded investigation into a duly elected official be any less ethical than the means employed by the Red Farm. Perhaps the Donkeys calculated that their method was more palatable than Sly's method. Perhaps they thought Shrill would win and their nefarious activities would never be exposed. Perhaps they expected that the crap-stained boomerang they threw at Pete would fly over his camp, dump its dirt, and return clean instead of returning with more dirt and dumping on them. Perhaps the pendulum would never swing back. Perhaps the tide would never reverse, perhaps, perhaps, perhaps.

Regardless what they believed, their method stunk inside and out. No matter how you sliced it, it still boiled down to a select group of individuals trying to overthrow an elected official solely for the reason they believed they knew what was better for the farm and that Pete was a bad animal. How ironic that they accused the Red Farm of meddling in the Rainbow Farm election, yet they meddled in their own election. Surely the sanctimonious Rainbow Farm would never do such a thing. They would never try to change the results of any election much less their own. They had never done such a thing. They were known as the Shining Farm on the Hill. One could easily argue what was happening on the Rainbow Farm did not stink any less than what the Red Farm had done.

Another difference was the number of innocent animals that inevitably get caught up in these types of activities. Straight out of the Red Farm playbook, "The ends justify the means." Different methods, same results. How could one method be worse than, or better than, the other? Justice the bull was in wait and would prevail. He would continuously buck the sanctimonious Rainbow Farm riders in their rhinestone suits who were desperately attempting to legitimize their illegitimate activities. Straight into the pig sty they would fly, ending up covered in muck and crap head to toe.

Observing the Rainbow Farm's follies, Sly and crew had a nice laugh at their expense. "Who's shining now?" cackled Sly.

"I think I can see a rhinestone shining through that crap-covered suit," said another.

So to use a saying from several sources, whether Ovid, Sophocles, or Machiavelli, and adopted by the Red farm, "the ends justify the means." Both farms wanted the same end; just their means were different. Paraphrasing one could profess that anything is acceptable if it leads to a successful result. Is it? Who is playing God in this scenario? Perhaps the original system, person, whatever one wanted changed, would have, could have worked in the first place if given a chance. Quite apparent that was never considered by these animals. No honeymoon for Pete, no grace period, no walking across the aisle. They hated him, and he had to go. Damn the Torpedoes.

A Canine, a Weasel, Fun and Games

DEVIL DOG

Who was this Devil Dog selected by the cabal? Why was he the best choice? Was he fair, would he be nonpartisan? Would the animals he selected to be part of his team be fair? Was his intent to expose the Red Farm or was it to expose Pete? What would his mandate be, what would the parameters be? So many questions. How long would it take? How conclusive would the findings be? Would his efforts and exorbitant amount of resources expended bring closure? Would his final report be the end-all, catch-all? Was this not the same animal that in a previous case left four innocent animals rotting in a pen where two of them died? He refused to right a wrong then; what made one think he would do the right thing now? Wasn't it ironic that the same bulldog who did right that wrong would be selected down the road to investigate the investigators and that their paths would cross again? Time would tell.

SHIFTY

The Weasel Shifty. What a piece of work the weasel was. Known as Shifty because he always had that look that indicated he was up to no good. During the entire investigation, Shifty would assemble in front of the farm and opine, "If you only knew what I knew but you can't know what I know because you can't see what I see because you are not as important as I am." For years, the myth of Santa and his annual visits on Christmas was real because all parents told their children that Santa really existed. He was real to the kids because someone in a position of authority; in this case, their parents told them Santa was real. They never saw him they just knew he existed because their parents told him he did, or the milk and cookies they left for him would be gone in the morning and there would be presents and everyone would be happy.

It was similar for Shifty. "Just wait for the Devil Dog's Report. I have seen firsthand examples of Pete colluding with Sly" as his eyes shifted back and forth. "I cannot tell you because that would violate my clearance. Just trust me." Just as Santa might promise a brand new ten-speed bicycle for Christmas, Shifty promised collusion. Shifty had seen the collusion firsthand and promised to the animals that just like the shiny, new bike the kids would get for Christmas, he would deliver as well. It would be state-of-the-art, all shiny, high speed, low drag and not only will you enjoy the ride, but it will also be the vehicle you need to allow you to successfully accomplish your ultimate objective of getting rid of Pete. Christmas Day (Devil Dog's report) comes, and you run downstairs all excited to see your new bicycle, and there it is a rusty frame unicycle with a flat tire. "Dang, Shifty, you are a deceiving Weasel. What is this?"

Shifty, instead of ceasing to dig, doubles down. "All is good, we have a Plan B!"

All Shifty's followers who believed in him so much weren't buying it. After the report was released and it was obvious to the entire farm that Shifty had pulled the wool over their eyes, he received a new name, the Fibster. But most still called him Shifty not just for his eyes but for the fact he shifted from one part of the farm to the other trying to avoid the Heckle Patrol who hounded him unmercifully wherever he slinked.

Fun and Games

There was a short lull after those first eventful days. Sort of a calm before the storm. Even though political differences and bickering in public seemed to be all Donkeys and Elephants could do, behind the scenes, they could come together and find common ground especially when it came to entertainment. They would set their differences aside and, on certain occasion, treat each other like animals. One of these events was the monthly Texas Hold 'Em game. In one game, in a sign of things to come, Shifty the Weasel and Jimmie the Wolverine were involved and were the last two standing. Jimmie had slightly more chips than Shifty, and in a daring move, Shifty went all in. Jimmie sized him up and knew he was bluffing. "You can't see what I have in my hand," Shifty said. "Trust me, I'm not bluffing. This is the real deal. I'm sitting here looking at a winner."

Jimmie, with no hesitation, replied, "Okay, Shifty." He had heard this story before. "I call" cards were laid down and Shifty had a nine-high nothing. Jimmie beat him with a pair of twos.

Another event that brought all the animals together was the annual farm rodeo. The main event that all watched as the grand finale was the bull ride. The Bull's name was Justice, and a tradition from the time the farm was first built was the bull-riding event. If an animal wanted to prove to the masses that he was seeking justice for the right reasons on his or her current crusade, then this was the best way to prove it. Stay on Justice for eight seconds was the requirement. Anyone could attempt; few did. But in every group of all animals, there are always a few who through arrogance or stupidity believed they had justice on their side and could easily prove it. Others like the Orangutan stated, "I'm too old for this, but trust me, I know I'm on the right side." The fervor of the crowd was at an all-time high. The timing of this year's event with a plethora of animals making accusations against Pete laid the groundwork for what would be must-see theater. Oddly enough, there were no Elephants in this year's competition who had decided as a group they had nothing to prove and would sit this one out.

First in the queue was Shifty. He had purchased a rhinestone costume complete with cowboy hat and lizard skin boots. Justice would always size up his potential riders and chuckled to himself, "This will be an easy toss. Do they really think I will let a weasel ride me for one second, much less eight?"

All the Asses yelled in unison, "Ride him like you own him, Shifty, we believe in you."

The backdrop, like at every event where there was a free crowd, was Max perched on a fence cawing away, "Impeach Pete! Impeach Pete!" Shifty climbed on Justice and, in what would go down as the shortest ride ever, was tossed one hundred feet across the pen, flying like a weasel missile straight into the side of a pile of manure. The Elephants howled with laughter; even Donkeys were laughing. Regardless of political affiliation, it was funny to watch Shifty get torpedoed into a pile of poop.

Next up, Ed the Toad. Once again, Justice wasn't having any of it. "Is this the best you can get of this species? A washed-up Toad. At least find a young Bull Frog. Where's Jeremiah?" Ed at best looked a little scared as he approached the mounting station. Not sure if it was his constipation kicking in that caused his grimace or if he just looked this way all the time. But Ed had a strategy. He planned to hop once the ride began, decreasing his contact time with Justice, thus increasing his chances of making eight seconds. Some might say that was cheating, but truthfulness was not Ed's strong suit. The gate dropped. Justice started bucking vigorously, and for a few seconds, it appeared his strategy might work. But after three seconds, an ill-timed hop by the stubborn toad had him landing just as Justice gave his most vicious buck, and it was not a pretty sight. Old Ed, grabbing his privates, just slid off the bull and was dragged away by rodeo monkeys. Later, the defeated toad was heard whimpering to himself, "How did I get caught up in this sordid mess? I let that maniac giraffe and his lovebirds talk me into this mess, and here I sit, sore and unable to hop. For the foreseeable future, I will stick to my safe gigs and be a talking head for SNN and other networks. Speaking of gigs, I feel like I got gigged."

Two down, two to go.

Next was the walrus Naddie, Nads for short. If possible, he looked more ridiculous than Shifty. As he lumbered up to the mount station, the crowd roared. "Hey, look at Naddie, all dressed in black with a ten-gallon hat. What is that shiny object on Nad's lapel? Is that a star? Is Naddie a sheriff?"

Unable to climb onto Justice, he had solicited the help of his committee to help him get on top of Justice. And if one thought universal suffrage, marathons, and mountain climbing were ambitious endeavors, they all paled in comparison to lifting an overweight walrus onto a bull. How they struggled mightily to lift Naddie up into position. The sight of his colleagues trying to lift him onto Justice was just too funny a moment where again, Elephants and Donkeys heckled unmercifully.

"That is the most work I have seen these so-called public servants for the animals do in years," laughed the crowd. "Surely if you can get him up on Justice, he can stay there for the required time. No way to buck him, he is too heavy." But the portly walrus Naddie and his committee would never get their opportunity for him to ride that day. In a seldom evoked rule, he was disqualified for failing to mount in the allocated time. This rule had been used before, but in the past, it had always been for the animals who just at the point of riding Justice got cold feet and intentionally violated the time requirement. In the case of Naddie, it was simply for the fact he was too fat, and they could not get him up on the bull.

The crowd again laughed, both sides. "What next?" they roared.

"The fat lady has indeed sung," howled another. "What could possibly top this?"

Then in walked AC. This would be interesting to say the least. A giraffe riding a bull. The crowd became silent, and their interest was piqued. Of the three previous riders—well, two and one pretender—it was AC whom the crowd believed as having the best chance to ride Justice. Had he not been impartial in carrying out his duties? After all, it was AC whom Shrill had blamed for losing the election. And it was AC who had been fired by Pete. "Would the real AC please stand up? Are you left or right today, AC?" roared the crowd. AC was a strange case with spectators on both sides of the aisle wanting him to succeed and spectators on both sides wanting him to fail.

His self-proclaimed *The Maniac Giraffe* was stenciled on the back of a leather vest, and *TMG* was visible on his Stetson. Justice knew this would be the only serious ride he would have. AC indeed would be his toughest ride. He was in much better physical condition than the previous riders and was a very imposing specimen. The long-legged tough guy had special stirrups that allowed his long legs to remain off the ground once mounted. It was a sight to behold. AC, Leaky, TMG, whatever you wanted to call him, was confident and arrogant and was convinced he would ride Justice. But Justice knew something that the others didn't. AC had a habit of trying to ride both sides, left and right. Threading the needle might work in his day job but not with Justice. At the sixth second into the ride, Justice had determined that every two seconds AC would change sides. As AC went for his next left shift, the clever young bull dipped left as well, and AC fell off the mighty bull, and unfortunately, with his left leg still in the stirrup and right leg waving in the air, he was dragged around the pen by Justice. Finally, when the cloud of dust cleared and the rodeo monkeys were able to extract AC, he limped off. AC, like Ed the Toad, decided to let his mouth do all the work. Back to the talk shows. Flapping his gums was much easier than riding Justice.

What was learned that day was a slant on an old proverb, "Better to remain an idiot in question then to open your mouth and remove all doubt." The new one was "Better to be considered an untrustworthy cad participating in a charade than to try to ride Justice and remove all doubt."

Next!

CHAPTER TEN

Regan's Inferno

Regan Smelly was so excited. A beautiful Irish setter whose name wasn't because she smelled bad—quite the contrary, she smelled so good with her expensive perfume and was beautiful to boot. As the highest paid female journalist for the BOX Network, she had jumped ship and now worked for what many referred to as the Not Believable Channel but officially was known as the Nightly Broadcast Channel network, NBC. She would be taking a trip to the Red Farm for a coveted sit-down interview with Sly. These were few and far between opportunities for Rainbow Farm journalists, and she was tickled pink at the opportunity. Even more surprising was Sly's team had not even asked for a list of her questions. Were they so naïve and ignorant not to know who she was and how she would make Sly look bad just as she had done with Pete in the debates? Regan arrived at the Red Farm, and the first thing she noticed was the beauty of the Red Farm female animals. She was just one of many here on the Red Farm, unlike the Rainbow Farm where she was one in a million, always the most beautiful one in the room, not to mention the smartest. The other thing she noticed was just how different the architecture was on the Red Farm's Headquarters section. She had seen pictures, but upon seeing it for the first time, one marveled at the onion bulb towers. Regan was led into the room and seated and waited for Sly. Sly came in, and she noticed just how young and full of vigor he looked compared to former Red Farm leaders. Sly took a seat across Regan, and the next thing she felt was his piercing eyes. He seemed to be looking right through her, and it was intimidating.

SLY: Good morning, Regan. Welcome to the Red Farm, I look forward to the interview.

REGAN: Good morning, Mr. Chief. I have lots of questions and time is short, so I will get to the heart of the matter.

SLY: Proceed and you can call me Sly.

REGAN: Okay, Sly, why do you have military forces on the Oil Farm?

SLY: Why do you have forces on the Oil Farm and numerous farms throughout the lands, and why do you have forces parked right outside the gates of our farm, a stone's throw away?

REGAN: Is this the way this interview is going to proceed with you answering questions with questions?

SLY: Only if they are stupid and self-serving questions, think outside the Box, no pun intended against your former network.

Regan was flustered but was showing no signs outwardly. She would get Sly; she would paint him into a corner and expose his evil empire and their nefarious activity to the entire world.

REGAN: Okay, Sly, I will be more thoughtful with my questions. Sly, why do you have so many nuclear weapons?

SLY: As one of your former great chiefs with a name similar to yours once said, "There you go again." Why does the Rainbow Farm have so many? And furthermore, it was the Rainbow Farm in a time not so long ago that symbolically tried to remove a portion of the yellow stripe from its Rainbow and employed these weapons against a fellow farm. Let's put things into context here. You locked up species of the yellow ilk on your own farm into pens, your own citizens, and then attempted to obliterate their farm of origin.

REGAN: But that was necessary to end a great conflict!

Regan suddenly felt the tides had been turned and she was the one being interviewed.

SLY: And ours is to prevent a great conflict.

Regan conceded the point and decided to switch gears.

REGAN: You have a big divide between rich and poor on the Red Farm. Is that fair for all your citizens?

SLY: And the Rainbow Farm does not! Again, context. Your entire farm's existence is conceived on wrongdoing. Your manifest destiny was running off an entire species of the beautiful cardinal and forcing these beautiful, harmless, little red birds off their land. In the process of doing that, you destroyed their way of life and located them on reservations and raped their once pristine landscape. Might as well remove that red hue from your rainbow like you did with yellow. Soon, there will be no colors, just white. And certainly not black, the color of the species which one can argue was the cornerstone of the success of your farm. Success that was built on the backs of your animals of color sold to you from their farms of origin. You then enslaved them for free labor to finance the agrarian way of life on the southern portion of your farm. And lastly, our farm has been around much longer than yours. Our animals can trace themselves back countless generations to their ancestors on our farm. Your ancestors came from other farms. Your Rainbow Farm is founded on imperialism and what originated as a group of farms invading an existing farm all in the name of exploration, and at some point, the transplanted citizens, not wanting to pay taxes to a faraway king ruling over them as a colony, decided they would form a perfect union. That gives new meaning to the word *perfect*. So it was businessmen for self-serving purposes, not Rainbow Farm Founding Fathers for the good of their fellow animals who saw an opportunity to break away and start their own business or, as they bellowed, start a perfect union for we the animals. Look at your documents. We the animals. Who is *we*? Did they really believe all animals are created equally? Is that perfect union for all species and colors of animals? This is written by animals who owned farms successful through slave ownership. Do you not see the preposterousness of this argument? Clean up your own house, and while you are at it, kick in some reparations for an entire species of animal that carried you on their backs. You even enslave your own children, entrapping them with predatory loans for their continued education. They are then at the mercy of the perfect union with high interest rates. So you call yourselves the Rainbow Farm and champion diversity, yet not only do you discriminate against your neighbors, the burrows attempting to come to your farm as huddled masses, you even discriminate against animals on your own farm. Your beloved leader of the past spoke about a shining farm on a hill at the end of a rainbow with a pot of gold and how this dream was open and available to all animals. It's a lie, it's a broken-down shack on a hill with a colorless rainbow and a pot of manure. That's your perfect union and Rainbow dream.

Regan suddenly felt as if she was trapped in a vortex and being sucked into a place she had never experienced as a journalist or animal for that matter. She felt she had been lured into a street fight for which he was woefully unprepared. Sly was bleeding her out with a thousand cuts, and instead of worrying about not having enough time, she was now wishing the time would expire faster. She felt exposed, on the defensive, and had been completely thrown off her game. Time to switch gears.

REGAN: Sly, why do you find it necessary to meddle in our elections?

SLY: I never did, but your highest leader of the farm has a record of meddling on several farms. Did not Cam meddle in Limey Farms referendum to leave an economic union? Did not Cam make a visit to the Oil Farm and attempt to turn public opinion against Ben Nettie, leader of one of the newer farms in the region? Here's some advice—he who lives in a glass house should refrain from throwing stones. We are aware of your meddling in our elections. Do we cry after the fact? No, we inform our candidates, all of them, and we inform our people that there will be misinformation out there, and we actively counter such nonsense? Did you warn all your candidates, especially the one you are trying to take down? Finally, if your constituents are influenced by fake personas on social media, you have bigger problems than who wins the election. And I will add emphatically, it was a pejorative process involving big fat Rainbow Farm thumbs and claws on the scales of justice, your own animals! You accuse us of meddling, you meddled against yourself. One party against the other. Donkeys fighting Elephants and Donkeys going after Pete. That would never happen on the Red Farm. And let's say— and I am speaking hypothetically—if we did meddle, it was just business as usual and just a small match starting a small fire. Instead of quickly putting out a small brush fire with water, you instead threw gasoline on it and it turned into a raging inferno. That inferno has raged since your election involving an exorbitant amount of resources and time that could have been spent on the business of the people instead of endless investigations and time wasted on fighting each other. Total gridlock.

REGAN: But people on your staff are identified as meddling!

SLY: I have thousands of animals working on my staff, and you single out one like it reflects the entire farm. One of your former chiefs had a statement, "The buck stops here." We do not operate that way. The buck stops with stupid and should not be a generalization applied to our farm and leadership. I advise you to find this person and ask him what his personal motivations and reasons for your so-called characterization of the entire Red Farm meddling in an organized fashion. Every barrel has some bad apples.

REGAN: Why are your forces abroad and present on other farms that are near the Rainbow Farm? What are your intentions?

SLY: Again, context. You have entered into an agreement with several farms near my farm. You are not only conducting combined military training and exercises just outside the fences of our farm. You have even stationed permanent forces just a stone's throw away. What are your intentions? Years ago, I can remember a gentlemen's handshake when immediately after hard times for our farm after we lost several territories, you agreed to not expand your own military unions at our expense. But no, you kicked us when we were down and invited seven smaller farms right up to our fence posts taking away our buffer zones and strategic depth to defend ourselves, and you talk to me about troops abroad and our intentions. We have a military union as well. What if we, through expansionist desires, invited farms in your periphery to join our military union and then set up camp just south and north of your borders? Again, what are your intentions? Before you even ask—because I can see the question forming in your little beautiful head—why we seized territories in our region. Well, we are more than willing to return seized territories to so-called rightful farms if you will do the same. Your entire Steer Belt was stolen from the Brown Farm. Give it back before you preach to us about giving back territories that historically belonged to us in the first place. Also, give us back certain territories you swindled from us north of your farm outside your boundaries.

Regan tried to avoid looking at her watch. When would this end? It was like looking at an hourglass or watching paint dry. At the back of the room, Sly's staff had set up a large hourglass to track the time for the interview. She found herself praying that the grains in the hourglass could fall faster and that the aperture would widen, and the grains of sand would slip through more rapidly. It was as if Sly had complete control somehow communicating to individual grains of sand when to and when not to pass through. Even more importantly, how did she look? Was he noticing her squirm? Was her makeup holding out? She felt hot and was having hot flashes. Please let this end. She decided to change course and take a softer approach, maybe talk more softball issues like family, patriotism, anything to burn time. Perhaps an innocent question would stop the bleeding.

REGAN: Sly, do you feel your farm animals are patriotic and loyal to your farm? Are you open to visitors on your farm?

SLY: Obviously more than yours are. Recently, I recognized one of our sports team who won first place in a universal competition. We gathered in a stadium along with all the farm animals, as many as could physically occupy the spaces. I led them in singing our Red Farm Anthem and every farm animal there to include the athletes stood and sang along, proudly displaying their pride of country and loyalty to the farm. Compare that to the image of your overpaid and spoiled athletes, the kneelers who refuse to even stand for the Rainbow Farm Anthem. Oh, say can you see? "Not from down here," they respond. Perhaps they take notice their color is not even portrayed in your proudly displayed rainbow. Isn't it interesting to you that most of those kneelers are people of color? And you question me on patriotism. I've seen your fickle and short-lived displays of patriotism. I've seen your so-called patriots who sell out your farm all in the name of money or trysts with members of the opposite sex, and you question the patriotism of our farm members. I assure you, we are alive and well and more patriotic then we have ever been. Go back home and ask your own citizens how they feel about the Rainbow Farm. Seems to me you are the ones with issues among your rank and file with respect to loyalty and love of country. As far as visitors are concerned, funny you ask me about being good hosts and welcoming to visitors on our farm. How are you on that front? What's up with that fence and this ridiculous fixation on hats and their symbolism. What's in a hat? You profess to be open to the huddled masses. Recently in your capital, you had a group of deserters from the Yellow Farm, who having deserted Rocket Land, a system of tyranny, came to the Rainbow Farm, and it being their first time there, they decided to—oh my god—buy MFGA hats. These completely innocent animals had escaped to what they perceived to be the Farm of the Brave and the Free and engaged in the first ever of their lifetime's capitalist exchanges, and what was their reward? Not "Welcome to our farm." No, they were verbally attacked and then physically attacked as the hats were jerked off their heads. Sounds like assault to me. Is that any way to treat a visitor? Maybe you should add a few words to your famous Mother Hen statue inscription. Perhaps it should read, "Your huddled masses yearning to breathe free, the wretched refuse of your teeming shore. Send these, the homeless, tempest-tost to me, I lift my lamp beside the golden door!" *Unless you have a MFGA hat on.* What is it with your Rainbow Farms and primal reactions that red hats seem to cause? Is that the next color to go on the rainbow? Pussy hats, red hats, white cone hats, hats of all size and shapes seem to bring out visceral reactions with you people. Here on the Red Farm, we have hats. We use them to keep our heads warm. And if

someone came to our farm and bought a hat, we would
say "Thanks, come back again, and spend some more
money." No, but the great capitalist of the world fences
off and harasses their customers.

REGAN: What about your protection forces? There are reports
your youth are in bad shape, not healthy?

SLY: And there are reports that the Rainbow Farm forces are
running out of qualified recruits. Over 70 percent of
your young animals are physically unfit for service. Your
joystick warriors who eat while they so-called fight can't
match our youth. Your gene pool of recruits is drying
up.

Regan was almost home. *Lord, help me reach the finish line*, she
thought to herself. Time enough for one more question. Perhaps she
could end on a positive note and escape out of the room with an
ounce of dignity remaining.

REGAN: Are you concerned about what Pete Junior said, "Red
Farm makes up a pretty disproportionate cross-section
of a lot of our assets"?

SLY: I don't care what Junior says. All I care is what Senior
says. It's been my pleasure, Regan, have a safe trip back
to your beloved Rainbow Farm.

And with that, Sly let her off the hook.

Regan would later say it was the worst interview she had ever
conducted. She had been handled and was obviously in way over her
head in her interview with Sly. Sly was brilliant. In this genuine way,
he came across incompetent when that approach served him. While
Sly pretended to be incompetent, Pete was the opposite; he pretended
to be competent and was incompetent. In contrast, Sly pretended to
be incompetent but was very competent. "He ran so many circles
around me I felt as if they started to close in on me, encircling me.
Starting at my legs and proceeding to my arms and chest I found it
hard to breathe. The constriction stopped at my neck, just enough

to allow me to continue to speak. I found it more difficult to pursue a hard line of questioning and the words without conviction feebly omitted from my mouth. I was quickly dispatched and found myself in a defensive posture rather than offensive. It was the longest hour of my life. There is a reason they call him Sly. That is one smart fox."

Welcome to my world Regan

CHAPTER ELEVEN

Willie, the Report, a Balloon Crash and the Inquisition on the Hill

The waiting is the hardest part. Everyone who believed what Shifty was telling them daily and really believed they would be getting a shiny new bike for Christmas were just literally dying with anticipation. This report would be the end of Pete. They believed what Shifty told them; they believed what was reported. Why, one might ask, because they hated Pete and they wanted it to be true? Emotion and hate tend to get in the way of facts. If presented with indisputable facts, how would the posse that had been after Pete since his election react? Would the report be conclusive or carefully crafted in a nebulous fashion to intentionally not bring closure thus keeping the narrative alive? This new front would undoubtedly be obstruction.

Facts were not important for the moment and the not-so-recent past as the Anti-Peters had some success slinging arrows of innuendo and gossip toward Pete, his family, and anyone associated with him. Also included as targets were the voters labeled as racist and deplorable just because they had voted for Pete or were part of his administration. But with every controversy, there comes a time that facts do become important and have the final say over all things. The mob, posse, and haters knew that time had arrived. Oh, how they wished and prayed that when the report was released, they could transition from their baseless accusations and exclaim in glee, "See, it's right there in the report, its factual, Pete cooperated with the Red Farm to take down Shrill." That would be the nail in Pete's coffin. They would finally have proof. So they anxiously waited. "There must be fire where there is smoke. Shifty and the *Gazette* told us so." And the waiting continued.

Finally, the report was released, and Willie, a tenacious bulldog and the new top cop of the farm says, "Wait a second. My team and I must prepare the report for all the animal's availability. That requires by law that I cover some things up." Willie also by law was not required to release the report at all. Pete have given the green light because of the high public interest in the case, and he felt releasing a redacted version would bring closure. Little did he know that it wasn't about the report at all. This was about him and the next election.

A little more on Willie. Thirty trips around the sun had transpired since Willie had last served as the top cop on the farm. He was not some rookie, some partisan hack like previous top cops. He was well-respected and frankly did not need the headaches and downside of taking this position. Simply put, he was the right animal for the right time to right the ship. He had decided that right was right and that the Rainbow Farm animals were entitled to see what their government officials were doing or had done in this sordid affair. In the spirit of transparency and knowing the masses wanted to know the gist of the report, Willie issued some key findings he made. He did not paraphrase, he did not summarize; he just provided key findings of the report: Firstly, did Pete cooperate with the Red Farm to interfere in the election, and secondly, was Pete guilty of obstruction? The revelation was a resounding no to both of those, and that was confirmed when the report became public weeks later.

Every day on the farm, you could look up and see the Collusion Balloon. Basically, it was an Anti-Pete platform flying above the farm with *C&O* (collusion and obstruction) stenciled on the side. Hanging from the side of the basket was Shifty armed with his bullhorn, who was repeatedly like a broken record saying over and over,

"Just wait and see, Pete colluded, Pete obstructed." Flying just below the balloon were Max and Leila with a banner reading *Impeach Pete* and, instead of their normal caw, were doing a CO call, "CO, CO, CO, impeach Pete!" The release of the Devil Dog report that day was a sight the animals would never forget. There is a saying "The air has left the balloon," which basically means you have run out of Schlitz; you have effectively been proven wrong. This day it happened both literally and figuratively when Willie released the report. As if by divine intervention on the CO, the fire fizzled out and the remaining helium dissipated, and the balloon began to descend rapidly.

What a sight to see as the entire group desperately tried to keep the CO from crashing and burning. "Quick!" shouted Shifty. "Lift up Naddie. Surely his flatulence can buy us some time." But it was not enough. The balloon came crashing down, and it was not a pretty sight. Naddie had landed on top of Shifty and broken his pencil neck. AC was on his back long legs flailing in the air. Fancy and Shrill were laid out flat, surrounded by pieces of the broken jug they had been sharing, both clinging to the handle. Caesar who had climbed the lines connecting the basket to the balloon had somehow ended up inside the balloon and was screaming to AC and Ed, "Get me out of here. You got me in this mess, now get me out!" Poor Max and Leila. Instead of being smart enough to let go of the banner and simply fly to safety, they hung on to each end for dear life. The result was the basket landing squarely on the banner, catapulting the two old birds right through the outside skin of the balloon on the inside with a flailing Caesar. As Caesar was trashing around on the inside of the balloon, he kicked both birds, and again, as if by divine intervention, their two beaks pierced the side of the balloon and their little heads stuck through with Max positioned over the C and Leila over the O. A spectator to this hilarious event was quoted and it stuck: "The Collusion and Obstruction is no more. C&O must now stand for Cantankerous and Obstinate."

Asses have their ass handed to them again

Poetic justice, the only one with no injuries was Rex, who never thought this was a good idea in the first place and only went along because Shrill said she would beat him with her newfound hammer if he didn't.

On the ground nearby, rolling around in laughter, was Justice, who bellowed, "Some animals never learn."

One would think after that day that this group would have reasoned and adhered to a proven directive "When you find yourself in a hole, stop digging." No, they proceeded to untangle themselves from each other, pulled Caesar from the balloon, found some new shovels, and commenced to digging. Shifting gears, they were now focused on obstruction. Seems Justice was correct; some animals never did learn. So that is where it stood. Not going after Pete for something he did not do but instead going after him for obstructing an investigation into something he did not do.

Meanwhile back on the Red Farm, Sly could not help himself as he and his cronies toasted to the Rainbow Farm. "Can you believe these idiots are giving us overtime? I thought for sure it would be over with the Devil Dog's report. One little match strike and I have had these imbeciles throwing gasoline on the fire for two years, and now, when it should be over in the midnight hour, they with a rebel yell are giving us more, more, and more. God bless you, comrades, for taking what you have for years rally cried as your strength, your sanctimonious diversity and turning it on yourselves."

Willie gave an impromptu interview in which he said, "Every show, every book, every plot, begins with an original thought. Someone, somewhere, decided in their head to do something. An idea, a concept is born. There are many dominoes that one can point to in all this mess. We know for a fact that Sly and his motley crew from the Red Farm meddled in the election. That has been happening for years and took place in all previous and past elections on the Rainbow Farm. That domino is identified. The hidden domino is undetermined. Who was the catalyst, the keystone, the Mack Daddy of Dominoes that would seize upon what the Red Farm did do and then parlay that into a case against Pete and his campaign resulting in a never-ending investigation, innuendo, attacks on Pete, his campaign, his family?

"There are many dominoes in this sordid saga: fake dossiers, symbolic insurance policies, fake news, and apolitical animals serving in high positions of law enforcement who were supposed to check their political baggage at the door of their workplace and serve objectively as opposed to subjectively. But there was one key domino that was behind all of this. Who was this wizard behind the curtain? We do know that Nova told Mona there was an insurance policy, so therefore Nova must know who the underwriters of such policy were. How and where did the opposition assemble? Did they operate independently, or did they inform their bosses? How high did it go? Did the buck stop anywhere?

"Other questions beg to be answered. If Cam and his agencies knew that the Red Farm was meddling and targeting Pete, how come they never warned Pete and provided him with defensive briefings? What was the nexus between Red Farm meddling and Pete colluding with Sly? What was the reason the FBI decided to open a counterintelligence investigation? What was the reason for a Special Counsel? What was its purpose? Why did the previous top cop recuse himself? Was that so his deputy could initiate a special counsel? Why did Devil Dog select as members of his team those who were biased against Pete? Many of these were financial contributors to Shrill's campaign. Would there be process crimes?"

THE INQUISITION

All the animals had gathered. Today was the day Willie volunteered to testify on the Devil Dog Report at the big pile of manure known as the Hill to both the upper and lower house committees. Both high-ranking Elephants and Donkeys would have five minutes each to question Willie in what was commonly referred to as *The Grill on the Hill.*

Here were some of the ridiculous questions that day:

DONKEY: General, why, if you knew what was in the report would be released to the public, would you misrepresent what was in the report in a summary?

WILLIE: As you can see from the report, I didn't.

DONKEY: General, why can't we see all the report?

WILLIE: Because I don't want to break the law that your body passed.

ELEPHANT: General, you are a fine-looking bulldog. How do you maintain your good looks?

WILLIE: It comes naturally.

DONKEY: Why did you find no obstruction?

WILLIE: Because there wasn't any.

ELEPHANT: General, where did you get that beautiful collar?

WILLIE: My wife got it for me. Came from the Yellow Farm.

DONKEY: General, do you think I look like Spartacus?

WILLIE: No. I think you look more like Shaft, and that is a compliment.

ELEPHANT: General, why did you decide there was no obstruction?

WILLIE: Two reasons. Firstly, of all the instances of what Devil Dog proposed as possible obstruction, not one of them met the definition of criminal intent which was required for a ruling of obstruction, just did not reach the bar. Secondly, it had to be me. Devil Dog passed it over, and after two years' time and an exorbitant amount of spent resources investigating this matter he did not make the call, so it had to be me.

After hours of this back and forth of a combination of ridiculous questions, grandstanding by candidates for the next election, and frivolous questioning from the Elephants, a question was finally asked that would set the chamber of fire and be the catalyst for what one might refer to as the unpeeling of the onion.

Donkey: General, do you think there was spying on Pete and his campaign?

Willie: I do think there was. Whether it was warranted or not is the question? I intend to find out if it was or not and get to the bottom of how this all started. And *spying* is not a dirty word. It's what these agencies do, and for good reason. However, it is how they go about it that is the question. Individuals—and yes, that includes Pete—as written in the Almanac have certain unalienable rights. I will investigate to find out if those rights were violated. And not just for Pete but any other animal on the farm.

It was as if Willie had reached in his vest and pulled out a vial of Holy Water and tossed it on the panel. Those possessed with the Anti-Pete bias immediately began to squirm and howl. This was about to get real. Somewhere behind closed doors watching from afar were the toad, giraffe, and orangutan. Ed, AC, and Caesar, as if on cue, muttered in unison a silent "Ruh Roh."

One would have thought that after this lengthy questioning by the higher body that the lower body would have been satisfied. The rank-and-file animals were satisfied. They had experienced enough of this ridiculous saga from their leaders and were ready for their government to get on with the business of the farm. But not Naddie and his gang. He wanted a second chance to prove he was on the right side of justice. "I know if I could just have gotten up on Justice, I could have stayed there for eight seconds and proven to all the animals just how righteous I am. This will be my chance, and Willie must now come into my house, my chamber, I'm the new Justice."

But again, Naddie would not get an opportunity to shine. To change the rules of the process and have lawyers question Willie instead of his panel members backfired and nixed Naddie's opportunity. Once again, the fat lady was singing for Naddie. Why did Naddie do this? Either he lacked the confidence in his panel to ask tough questions and represent adequately, what they were elected to do, or he was setting a trap to get Willie on a perjury charge. Wille was having none of it. He refused to play along, and my goodness, how the wailing began.

"He's hiding something," crowed a crow.

"He is a liar," clucked a hen.

"Who does he think he is? We have oversight responsibility!" cried another.

"Is he afraid? Is he chicken to appear?" snorted a pig. What took place next would be one of the more absurd chapters of this entire affair. Naddie still had the hearing, but it was to an empty chair.

One pig named Jowls, from the Donkey Party, was from a mound of manure known as Orange Mound. (There were several large mounds of manure on the farm, and over time, as they became unsightly, it was decided to paint them different colors.) Jowls, to ridicule Willie, brought a ceramic chicken inside the chamber. If that wasn't disrespectful enough, he even was eating fried chicken in the chamber. This unforgettable incident should provide excellent fodder for his future opponents. "Here is how Jowls represents you. He goes to the Rancid Pond and stuffs his fat face with fried chicken on your dime!" Anyone running against Jowls could say that and they would not be fibbing. So the entire morning was déjà vu all over again as representatives challenged an empty chair. A repeat of the same accusations and banter that the higher body had just recently conducted. Watching again with glee was Sly.

Sly said, "They point fingers and accuse other farms of being authoritarian regimes ruled by dictators or the few. Look at what is happening on the Rainbow Farm. A select few on powerful committees and in high-level positions are bringing the entire farm to a standstill over something that never happened. The animals and their basic needs are being ignored all because these hucksters on a wild goose chase are hungry for power and mainly because they hate Pete. Some system. Damned be the animals—who cares about them?

Never have I gotten more bang for the buck than this has provided. These clowns spent millions that could have been put to better use, and what did they get? They proved we meddled. We have been meddling for years; like playing slots, we do it again and again. Usually with a small return but this time, *triple* sevens. It never was about proving we meddled. That could have been easily proven without all the rigmarole. It was about the takedown of a duly elected official. And they went all in. The so-called volumes of their final report. How could there be Volume 2 if Volume I clearly demonstrated there was no crime? Thousands of trees sacrificed for that garbage of a report. These are great times on the Red Farm."

CHAPTER TWELVE

WOO Hoots

ELLIE: Good evening. I am Ellie Madcow here live with the Shrill News Network. Today we will be interviewing what many refer to as the Wise Old Owl, or simply WOO for short, on the mess we find ourselves in here on the Rainbow Farm. Wise One, thank you for coming down from your perch to share your perspectives with us on what can best be described as a tangled web we have woven. We look forward to your thoughts and insight. Did other farms meddle in our election, and should we be concerned? Why do you think Pete won and Shrill lost the election? Who were his voters?

WOO: Thanks, Ellie, you can call me WOO. Yes, we need to be concerned about all other farms and their meddling in our elections, but our real concern is how we behave ourselves. The Rainbow Farm and anyone on it is on shaky ground when it comes to slinging arrows at our adversaries for meddling in elections. We have done it in the past as well. To then act all sanctimonious and point at our adversaries and say stop—well, my friend, what's good for the goose is good for the gander. Let's police ourselves. Furthermore, to then use that meddling from the Red Farm as a vehicle or tool and go after a duly elected official just because we despise his looks, his character, the way he talks, the fact that he was an outsider was, well, to be frank, juvenile, stupid, and exactly what Sly wanted.

Have you ever considered the accusation that Sly wanted Pete to be elected and had it in for Shrill? What benefit would Sly get from a Pete administration over a Shrill administration? Pete was a complete unknown, and after all, it was Shrill, Cam, and the Donkeys that had attempted rapprochement with the Red Farm. Pete was not even in power. Pete never made a trip with a red reset button to the Red Farm. Pete was never caught on a hot mic like Cam telling Sly's colleagues that he, Cam, would have more flexibility once he was reelected. Had it not been past administrations of the Elephants that had traditionally taken hard lines with the Red Farm? Why the sudden switch? As to why Shrill lost? Shrill was a terrible candidate and ran a terrible campaign. Pete was not your ideal candidate either, according to many polls. So you have a wash there. Therefore, the next determining factor is who ran a better campaign. Well, I think you know the answer to that one. Also, Shrill did not listen to Rex. Apparently, she never learned anything from him. Rex was so likable. His charisma was intoxicating, and when he walked into a room, he owned it. Shrill was the exact opposite. But it is not simple as that. There are other more relevant reasons when you do an autopsy of the election that come to light. The win was less about Pete, more about voters' dissatisfaction with Shrill as a candidate and more of a rejection of what in effect would have been a third term of the Cam ilk. The Swing Belts spoke loud and clear.

WOO: Who were those who voted for Pete and why did they vote for him? Doesn't take rocket science to analyze this group of voters and to determine they were animals from all parts of the farm, animals of different species, animals of different sexual preference, different-colored animals voted for Pete. To stereotype them all as uneducated and part of a group of Deplorables is prejudicial and reeks of the hypocrisy of the left. One of the sacrosanct rules of politics is do not concede votes to your opponent. Shrill's Basket of Deplorables' description of Pete's supporters and threatening to put miners out of work were huge no-nos. Other Pete supporters could, surprise, walk and chew gum at the same time and could be characterized as multi-issue voters. They were those who had the vision to see that there would be openings on the highest court of the farm and wanted elephants to fill those vacancies. Regardless if Pete was a good candidate or bad, if he won, he would make those appointments. Back to the miners and others who had been identified as possessing jobs that Shrill considered a thing of the past. Shrill telling them "I will put you out of business" had to be what can only be labeled as a stupid thing to say. Other workers in other industries like the chickens on the farm had to wonder, "Am I next on the chopping block?" Juxtaposition her comment of deplorables and taking away jobs on top of Pete's promise to protect those jobs and lift barnyard regulations to create new jobs and to control access to the farm from those who might take away jobs and to make the farm grow again. And finally accept the fact when faced with choices, good or bad candidates, animals have their own prerogative to vote for who they want and guess what you may be surprised by who they select. That doesn't make them a racist, or a bad animal, they just are animalistic and, like humans, have preference. Put all these different pieces together and the conglomerate is a significant number, a significant enough voting block to win an election.

ELLIE: WOO, you have been around a long time and seen many things. Is this the worst you have seen it on the farm?

WOO: Yes, by far, there used to be a time when you could walk around the farm and keep your feet clean, now everywhere you go, your chance of stepping in manure is high probability. It's as if snipers contracted by both Donkeys and Elephants are hired hands, character assassins with crap guns who are engaged in high-intensity crap slinging. You can't make it from one side of the farm to the other without being hit by these turd bullets. And this is just small arms. Other larger Kaka Delivery Systems, KDS, litter the once pristine beautiful landscape of the Farm with piles of crap. Just the other day I witnessed what should have been a five-minute straight walk to the well turn into a one-hour trip. A poor goose in Mission Protective Posture and carrying an umbrella to protect herself from fallen projectiles zigged and zagged through what is a minefield just to go to the well. Society is perplexed, up is down, down is up, black is white, white is black, can't refer to a doe as a doe and a buck as a buck, no winners, no losers, just participation trophies, safe spaces, Almanac is being read upside down, legislators judge, judges legislate, yada, yada, yada. It really has become confusing. To the point where pragmatism is labeled as racism. There are so many new offensives and unfounded fears we need new -isms and -phobes to capture them all.

ELLIE: What are your views on Pete and his determination to build a fence and control the flow of illegal animals into the farm?

WOO: Not to answer a question with a question, but what is a fence normally designed for in a practical sense? There have been thousands of fences built around the world, yet it is this one that seems to get all the press. On the Yellow Farm, they have a huge fence that has been around for years. Not to say all fences are good. Some fences have been designed to keep animals in, and in that case, it is wrong, it is a pen with fences. Our farm has always been open to immigrants and the diversity they bring to our farm. However, there is a downside to completely open borders to the farm. Not every animal that comes on our farm comes for a good reason. There will always be groups of bad actors that under the guise of coming to the farm for good purposes come with the intent to do harm. Others sneak across like snakes slithering in the night undetected. Are they all bad snakes? Well no, they are not. Are they all good snakes? Well no, they are not. What are their intentions for coming into the farm? Are they all good, all bad? Well, somewhere in between, meaning by percentage alone, there will be some bad actors. Well, let's just say they are all not King Snakes, the most loved snake on the Farm. Times have changed, and what used to be a practical reason for the normal standard of accepting more as opposed to less has changed over time. Other practical and truly legitimate reasons to stem the tide and decrease the flow is that the population of the farm is not as it once was, very small and in need of influx. That does not make one's proposal for an adjustment to current rules and laws a racist. It makes him a pragmatist. But we live in a new world, there are new domains that will require other types of fences in the virtual world. Will there be as much commotion to barriers we cannot see as there is for the old-fashioned fences? But is this big push by the donkeys for open borders for truly benevolent reasons? If so, I challenge those who profess such benevolence to hike your butt right on down there and jump on Justice. You cannot deny that the real reason of many politicians is to flip regions and belts so that they improve their chances of getting elected in future elections.

ELLIE: Are these the worst or best of times?

WOO: Yes and yes. There have been challenging times and legitimate -isms that divided our farm, but this is different. And although a very challenging time it has been a very rewarding time as well. Look at the success of the economy. Unemployment down, there are good things taking place.

ELLIE: Can you provide examples? And please explain how it is different this time around.

WOO: Recent and not so recent, such as the election where because of the vote count from the Gator Belt, it took intervention by the highest court in the land to determine who the winner was, or who can forget the riots where portions of the farm literally burned, or when four protesting university students were gunned down by our own interior forces? But these were movements generated at the grassroots, and our leaders were able to eventually resolve these problems. This feels different where many high-ranking public officials generated at the higher levels of government this controversy we find ourselves in today. What is so perplexing is that when threatened by adversaries we normally come together, but in this case, when everyone agrees that the Red Farm interfered in our election, we have turned on one another instead of them. I am sure the Red Farm and Yellow for that matter are eating this up.

ELLIE: How would you characterize this gridlock, this controversy?

WOO: It is no doubt one of the most sordid affairs in the short history of the Rainbow Farm and on both sides of this equation one can find dirt. High-ranking personnel of the political apparatus of the Farm have been exposed for engaging in nefarious activity. Investigative bodies were obviously used by one party against the candidate of another party. Character assassinations seemed to have reached a new high, or low, depending how you look at it. Let's just say high in quantity, low in how far they would sink to attack innocent animals to sell a narrative. It stinks, and it's made us a laughingstock to other farms, especially the Red Farm, which is reveling in our self-inflicted misfortune.

ELLIE: WOO, How did this all begin, why did it happen, and why does it continue?

WOO: Separate questions. I will address the second one first: Why did it happen? Simple answer, the Donkeys who were so cocksure they would win but lost. This entire sordid affair was an attempt to assassinate the character of a duly elected official and overturn the results of a fair election. The Donkeys' strategy backfired. They gambled that Pete winning the Elephant nomination and knocking out the real competition was a godsend for their candidate. Their rationale was that someone with no political experience could not possibly beat out their candidate who had experience and was not only loved by the left but more organized and had more money. As the general election campaign progressed and the obvious flaws of Shrill became more front and center the why seed was planted. One could argue on merit that the system used for electing the CoF was outdated and needed updating and that the Eggtorial College was not fair to candidates who won the popular vote but lost the election. Sour grapes are one thing, amending the constitution is another, but the other part of who and how, an attempted coup which was much darker and nefarious, was a threat to democracy on the farm. Another fact is that what happened before the election would never have seen the light of day if Shrill had won the general election. Do we really think all the noise about Red Farm collusion would have seen the light of day if Shrill had won? Pete winning had second and third order effects exposing the corrupt underbelly of the Rainbow system. The time lag between Pete taking office and Cam still controlling the government was a period of about one hundred days where the Cam administration was still calling the shots and they faced a serious dilemma. Either sit and wait for Pete to discover what they had done, which he undoubtedly would do, or go all in on damage control. Can you imagine on election night when the Brutus clan watched nervously as Pete racked up electoral votes? Can you feel their heart rate increase and blood pressure go up once Pete won the Badger and Dairy belts? In their minds, they saw the tsunami forming out at sea that would sweep in and expose all of them. "Time to cash in that insurance policy, time for plan B, God help us," they must have muttered.

ELLIE: Do we know who the animals behind this were?

WOO: Where there is smoke, there is fire. And some of these fire starters self-immolated. The ones that really received mass coverage on the radar screen was the pillow talk between Nova and Mona. Others, by their actions self-identified as well. The question is how much higher it goes. It's high already.

ELLIE: Why would so-called smart and intelligent animals engage in such behavior?

WOO: Good question. Why not suck it up and wait until the next election for legitimate change is another good question. Pete was not a threat. He could easily be dispatched at the polls in the next election. Small groups of very powerful animals on the farm to include Caesar, the Toad, Nova, and the Giraffe were the real threats to democracy. Character assassination is the chosen sport on the farm when it comes to politics, and these so-called gentlemen exceeded the parameters of their positions, abandoning their apolitical mandates for the political arena. Their actions after leaving their respective offices speak louder than any words. They became pawns and useful idiots of a mainstream press that over 90 percent of the time ran negative stories on Pete and his administration. Why would these men with, up to that point, scandal-free careers do this? Easy answer. Power. Power tends to corrupt; absolute power corrupts absolutely. As power increases, a person's sense of morality lessens. A judgment on their morality will bear out, but the speculation they were involved in nefarious activity is a safe bet. Another part of why is one that bothers the public more than most other reasons the arrogance of these animals who really believed they were smarter than your rank-and-file animals on the farm? Not only smarter but they believed they were morally superior as well. They, not you, knew what was best for the farm. After all you were deplorable, uneducated coal miners, farmers, and factory workers. You clung to God, guns, and religion. They would make things right at your expense. My friend, if that is not an attempt at voter disenfranchisement, then I am not sure what is.

ELLIE: Do we know how this all began?

WOO: Well, Ellie, some of this is pure speculation, but I can present a scenario that I personally think is not far from the truth. Whether it was one fire starter or multiple with different agendas that started separate fires that combined into one raging inferno is the big mystery. Was Sly brilliant and Machiavellian enough to realize the bang for the buck he would receive from his business as usual meddling, or was it the high-charged and contentious environment that was a perfect storm? We all know that all farms that are capable meddle in some sort or fashion in other farm's elections. One has to take recent history into account and ponder, did Sly really want an Elephant administration? Was it not the Donkeys under Cam who promised more flexibility, wanted a reset with relations, and considered the anti-Red farm policy as outdated and of the past not the future? Why would the Red Farm want an Elephant administration that normally takes a harder line with respect to the Red Farm?

ELLIE: Excuse me, WOO, the how.

WOO: Thanks for getting me back on track. Possibly real-world events or if you believe in conspiracy theories then events such as a bogus warrant allowing internal agencies on the farm to spy on our own animals here and abroad were all components of this. Imagine a room with high-level investigators, our top cops. Here is where the why transitions into how. "Well, we may lose, what should we do?" and "Well, we lost, here is what we do now. If you think you may lose, then you keep an ace in the hole," and that was Nova's insurance policy. We may never know who approached who, who gave approval, and how far up the chain it went, *but* we do know somebody did something. We do know that certain things happened. We do know that Nova told Mona not to worry there was an insurance policy. We do know that Nova said he could smell Pete supporters. And the really big thing we know is that Shrill and the Donkey Committee paid for opposition research. This was for digging up mud on Pete. That is what opposition research is. Both sides do it. But this was different in that an agent from another farm, the Limey Farm, contacted Red Farm officials for this information. Disinformation would be a more suitable characterization and passed this off to Fission GPS. And it would snowball from there. This information on the dossier was not vetted but used to snooker a judge to obtain a warrant to spy, surveil, watch undetected, whatever one wants to call it on Rainbow citizens on the farm and off the farm. There is more to this convoluted saga, but every stinking arm from the rotting head of this octopus cannot escape the fact that everything they do ties back to an ill-conceived and nefarious plot. The question remains, who was the head of this duplicitous mob? Was it Cam, was it Shrill, or was it the Orangutan, the Toad, the Giraffe, the lovebirds? Anyone's guess at this point. Hard to think that all the nefarious activity and acts that took place was an independent action.

Someone high up had to know due to the seriousness of what was taking place, and the assets needed to conduct such activities. The logical conclusion is it went to the highest levels of the Cam administration.

ELLIE: Why does it continue? The Turkey Mac said it was Case Closed!

WOO: What is the "tempest raging o'er the realms of ice?" A tempest in a teapot. This will go down as the most exaggerated tempest ever on record, and to answer your question on why it will continue, there are many reasons. It is the nature of the beast, one whose arm attempts to break his legs and one whose fist punches itself in the mouth. Why? Because they can. They have the time that should be spent on legislation, yet they use it to squabble over nonsense. One why leads to another. Why? Because they can, because they hate Pete, because they hate the baby, they hate the father, they hate, hate, hate, and they cannot help themselves. It's what they do. While most animals are concerned about the next feeding these political animals spend their time pontificating and determining what is best, not for the masses but themselves. And it's not the first time. The Elephants did the same with Rex years ago. So invariably, what is best for the masses is superseded by what is best for them, and that is remaining in power. You are talking about animals on both sides of the aisle that were threatened by Pete. That was one group. Another was those that weren't threatened by Pete and wanted to demonstrate their support for him but were afraid. They were hedging their bets so to speak. In the early part of Pete's administration, there were Elephants that were afraid to stick their neck out because what if the salacious charges and allegations against Pete were true? Then that would mean they would join Pete on the chopping block and be perceived as guilt by association. In my humble opinion as the Wise Old Owl, this was never about the Red Farm wanting one candidate over another and being capable of influencing an election. Two points related to that. Firstly, even if they did want to influence an election, it was Cam who correctly made the point that the decentralization of the process would make that virtually impossible. Secondly, if our constituents are so fickle, ignorant of the issues, and malleable that their vote can be determined by misinformation and fake news, then we have other more serious issues internally. So the nexus was never there. In a concerted effort to take something, meddling, that had happened repeatedly over the years and then use that as a pretense for false accusations against a duly elected official, well, there is your crime. After two years of connecting the dots and trying to force the round peg into the square hole, the Donkeys have come up empty. You might say the Assess had their ass handed to them. So it was a big strikeout on collusion, yet that did not change the water temperature. In fact, it got hotter.

Cluck, cluck, cluck, went the Hens, switching gears and using Volume II of the Devil Dog report as fodder. "Pete obstructed!"

"Obstruction!" cried the Beavers as they slapped their tails in unison.

"Obstruction!" yelled the Kangaroos as they emptied their pouches and tossed rotten apples.

"Obstruction, obstruction, obstruction!" barked the Walrus, who immediately issued unwarranted subpoenas.

WOO: Consider this for a moment—Pete obstructed. Obstructed what? He obstructed nothing. It was left open in Volume II, forcing Willie to make the call and then occur the wrath of the Donkeys using it as an alternative to impeachment but serving the same purpose, bringing down Pete's administration and win the next election. If Pete obstructed anything then it was an obstruction of injustice. Here is where Pete's counter-punching that served him so well in the primary and general election worked against him in this ridiculous trap set by the Donkeys. Scenario follows, a shark in high office is accused of robbing a casino in the desert. Everyone knows it did not happen—impossible for a shark to get to Vegas and survive long enough out of water to make his way into a casino and rob it and pull off such a caper. The shark knows personally he did not commit this crime, and there is overwhelming evidence he never committed such crime. It's unfair, and being a shark, he acts out in a fit of anger and tells his fellow sharks to eat the investigators because he is innocent and this unfounded and untrue accusation is cramping his style. Although the shark himself could have legally eaten the chief investigator himself and had every right to do so, he did not. Additionally, his staff never ate the investigators as well. So please explain to me how the shark is guilty of obstruction for something that never happened. How can there be a Volume II when there is no Volume I?

ELLIE: What baby and what father are you talking about?

WOO: Devil Dog's report is the baby, and when they finally got to see the baby, they did not like what they saw. As the surrogate mother, Devil Dog passed off the baby to the rightful parent, Wille, who by law did not even have to release the report. He could have used it for toilet paper if he wanted. But to appease the rabid mob, Pete instructed Willie to release a redacted version, which would take some time to do properly adhering to the laws of the farm. In the meantime, Willie attempting to hold off the rabid mob released what he considered to be the gist and major findings of the report that there never was any cooperation with the Red Farm by Pete or any other animal from the Rainbow Farm for that matter. One would think that was good news and to be celebrated, correct? Willie also, with his deputy Stieny, a bespectacled opossum who initiated this entire affair, determined there was no obstruction as well. Again, good news, that there was no cooperation with the Red Farm and no obstruction, but no way. The Donkeys just kept digging and switched gears from collusion to obstruction. Here are questions I get asked from even the most simple-minded of animals who are the most pragmatic when it comes to looking at this. How can it continue? If there was no crime in the first place, then how can there be obstruction? What on earth is Pete supposed to be obstructing? If I know I am innocent and make attempts to prove that, is that obstruction? If I know I am innocent and get frustrated to the point of going after my accusers, is that obstruction. Again, it all is another example of how the Rainbow Farm is exactly like the Red Farm. Historically, the Red Farm was known for the phrase, which they put into practice of, "Show me the animal and I will show you the crime." Well, here we are on the Rainbow Farm, and is there any better example of that "Show me an animal, a candidate you hate who just happened to win, and I will show you the crime"? The report comes out, is redacted like all reports of this type have always been, and the donkeys continue to bray. What's under the blocked-out portions, we demand to see. So what happens when you don't like the message? You attack the messenger. You must give us the full report, they cry. You must appear before us, we have oversight. So Willie appears before the higher body and it is just character assassination from one side and glowing tributes from the other all over a report that has been released to the public. Especially predictable are those planning on running for election as next CoF—go figure, free air time. What happens next cannot be made up. The lower body then demands to see Willie, and at the last second, Naddie changes the rules so Wille decides not to attend, which was a voluntary visit in the first place.

WOO: Ole Naddie and his grandstanding mob have a conniption fit. Kabuki theater at its finest, they set out an empty chair and bring in a ceramic chicken to symbolize Willie is afraid and chicken to come see them. One disgusting creature from the Bluff City and orange mound a fat pig named Jowls brought food into those hallowed halls and stuffed his fat face. Next to Naddie, he was the last one who should be eating anything. It gets even more ridiculous. Now the butt-hurt committee have made Willie public enemy number one. They decide to hold him in contempt for not giving them a report that has already been released. Wille had made an unredacted version available to them that was only 2 percent redacted, and not one of the Donkeys accepted the offer and read the 98 percent unredacted version. So what does Naddie and his clowns do for the next circus act? They decide to hold Willie in contempt for not providing them something, a 100 percent unredacted version, which if he did would be breaking a law that they passed. I ran into the maintenance man, Marcellus, the other day and he was so frustrated by all this that he said, "If I could find my dang hammer, I would find a few thug hyenas and go into those chambers and go medieval on those Asses." One could only wonder what they could be accomplishing if they put the same amount of energy into doing right by the animals. Last thing I will say on why it continues. Purely political. They have no legislative achievements to hang their hat on, so they see this as the best way to go after Pete for the next election. Attack Willie as a proxy for tainting Pete. The other reason to go after Willie is because he is going to bring them down. Devil Dogs findings symbolize the swinging back of the pendulum and reverse path of the boomerang. After years of baseless accusations and promises of proving that Pete and his team worked with the Red Farm, they got nothing. The risks they took and laws they broke trying so hard to get this result and it didn't happen. They were the like the rats following the Pied Piper to their demise. The question remains, Who is the Pied Piper? In this version, it's a bit different. Not all the rats followed. Three that were able to escape the first purge remained behind and kept up the fight—one was lame, one was deaf and one was blind. One can only guess who these three were. Many fit that protype, but what comes to mind is the Walrus, the Crazy Bat, and the Farm Crier, or was it the Toad, the Giraffe, and the Orangutan?

ELLIE: What are your thoughts on Devil Dog? What would you ask him if you had the opportunity?

WOO: Some questions I would have for Devil Dog would be how soon in the process did you determine there was no collusion, no cooperation between Pete and the Red Farm. And once you determined that, would not any action by Pete not be applicable toward an obstruction charge? Once you determined there was no cooperation by Pete with the Red Farm, why not release that? What else was there left to do? Why hold our farm the Rainbow Farm hostage for all that time?

WOO: Especially troubling to me Devil Dog was why in your report, what is referred to as the gospel, did you leave open the question of collusion? Pete either obstructed against a crime that you determined he did not commit, by the way, or he did not. With all the resources at your disposal, you could not make that simple determination. You invented a new finding, not not guilty. Either Pete did and was guilty or did not and was innocent. But you passed the buck. Why did you care what the media thinks? Why pour gasoline on the impeachment fire and try to restart the narrative? Methinks you did it purposefully. Maintain the slow boil on Pete, provide unfounded bread crumbs for the Donkeys to make claims of obstruction, again for something that never happened. Pass the buck and put Willie on the chopping block. Make him make the bad guy for what was really a not-so-hard call or you would have made it in the first place. But you didn't because you did not want to be the bearer of bad news for the Donkeys. Lastly, why were there so many Donkeys on your special council, especially ones that donated to Shrill's campaign or, even worse, had track records of being defeated 9–0 by the Highest Court of the Land. Couldn't you have put together a better and more objective team? Oh, one more question from Marcellus. How can there be a Volume II if Volume I was a crock? "Gotta love those lay animals," laughed Willie.

ELLIE: I want to transition away from the election and talk some other issues about life here on the farm. As you are aware, there is a movement by certain black lions for reparations for the time they were slaves on Rainbow Farm. How do you feel about that?

WOO: The further removed we get from evil, it somehow sneaks back in a different form. There was a time on this farm when black lions from the Black Farm were sold as slaves to the Rainbow Farm. They were literally the lynchpin of the southern portion of the farm, the backbone of its existence. They were not allowed freedom of movement on the farm. As you know, we removed this cancer as an acceptable practice from the farm. Yet it sneaks back in other harder-to-detect forms. You now have massage parlors and clubs where animals from the Yellow Farm are entrapped not by literal chains and shackles but another type of confinement, economic dependence. How can that be acceptable? As for reparations, I am against it mostly for practical reasons. Firstly, it would be much too difficult to determine what the amount would and should be. Secondly, is it acceptable that animals be responsible for the sins of their father? Thirdly, we would give rebirth to the division that we painstakingly have moved past. Reviving that dark chapter and reopening it would sow discord and once again separate the animals by species. Time to forgive, not to forget, but forgive and move on. But oddly, the submarine Reparations surfaces every election year as the Donkeys start pandering to certain groups promising to make things right.

WOO: Immediately after the election, Reparations descends, but you know it's out there somewhere ready to ascend for the next election cycle.

ELLIE: What are your thoughts on all these new movements that seem to be taking place on the farm?

WOO: I will share with you a story I heard the other day. Every year there is a race called the Fastest Little Heifer. Not the Young Bull Sprint, the Fastest Little Heifer. So it's race day, the race is about to start, and among all the heifers on the start line is a young bull, Sam, with a ridiculous wig and fake udder attached to his underbelly. The racing official, a quick-witted mongoose who goes by the name Bennie Sharpy, says, "Sam, what in the world are you doing here, this is a race for heifers?" "I am a heifer now," says Sam. "No," says Bennie, "You are a bull in a ridiculous wig with fake appendages pretending to be a heifer." "You are anti-transgender!" screams Sam. "No, I am a race official that ensures fairness and that heifers race heifers, not bulls," says Bennie. These movements each have degrees of legitimacy, but many of the aspects associated with them border on the absurd. And like everything else there are downsides that end up hurting the ones they were designed to help. I will give you an example. There was an administration building where many hens and roosters were working. One of these movements was about the treatment of hens by roosters in the workplace. It was borne out by the accusation made by a hen against a rooster for something he did years ago. It ended up as substantiated, but when this occurred, that behavior was not perceived as crass as it may seem now. Back when it happened, the behavior was acceptable. Because of the hen and her case, a new movement was born, and more and more hens came forward with allegations many of which were not true and proven to be false, destroying careers in the process. As a result, in the workplace, roosters were afraid to even approach hens on the most trivial of matters. They were walking on eggshells. Production and morale went down. As a result, many owners of businesses decided not to not hire roosters but instead to not hire hens anymore. One may counter why not hire any roosters, but that was not possible because there were not enough hens available for the work required.

ELLIE: What are your thoughts on the investigative bodies charged with keeping us safe?

WOO: There were also several agencies created that worked in support of the Chief and on the behalf of all the farm animals. Many of these agencies are charged with investigating just about every facet of animal life one could imagine. Years ago, in one of the many conflicts between the Rainbow Farm and the Oil Farm, one of these agencies convinced the CoF that the Oil Farm was hiding a cache of pesticides intended for use against the Rainbow Farm.

WOO: After launching a full-blown invasion and takedown of the Oil Farm, they then looked for those stores of pesticides and found nothing. "Oh well, it needed to be done anyway," was their answer. This was not the first time they had an intelligence failure. After the horrible attack on the Rainbow Farm by Laddie, there was a demand for an autopsy to determine how the attack could have possibly succeeded. A special commission was set up to find out how Laddie was able to pull it off. How could twenty-one camels come to the Rainbow Farm living in plain sight hatch a coordinated plan that resulted in massive property destruction and loss of life on the farm? The main conclusion of the commission was that the separate agencies did not cooperate and share intelligence that could have prevented this devastating attack, the worst ever on the farm. These plots can either be discovered from a top-down approach or from very basic observations from the bottom. I will not get into all the findings but will summarize. There was a host of operational failures that were discovered during the autopsy. Lack of unity of effort and unity of purpose among the protection forces at all levels was the long pole in the tent. Joint intelligence work and sharing of information allow the separate pieces of the puzzle to be put together, and a common operational picture emerges. This did not happen. There are not technological barriers to this concept but cultural and institutional firewalls that need to be terminated for this to happen. How ironic that history and future events would clearly demonstrate that in the case of Laddie and the attacks on the Rainbow Farm, the cooperation of such agencies was nonexistent. But in the case of taking down Pete, a duly elected official and winner of the highest office on the farm, no stone would be left unturned in the efforts of these respective organizations' cooperation in planning, information, and operations. How sad!

ELLIE: What are your thoughts on today's youth on the farm?

WOO: Now back when I was a young owl, life was so much harder. I had to fly against a strong headwind to and from school. Before and after the school day, I had chores such as providing food for my siblings and finding new prey. You young owls of today are so spoiled. Now, Ellie, isn't that the story every generation hears from their parents? But there does seem to be some truth to what I would call the softening of our youth. Safe spaces, consolation trophies, being stopped in their tracks at the very first obstacle they encounter on a task—all of these are concerning. Now seriously speaking, when I was a young owl serving in the Barnyard Protection Services, I lived in a barracks with many other young owls. In our barracks, there was a room called a day room. That room had a pool table, card table, and games. It was the focal point of that building where all the young animals serving would gather routinely to socially interact. It fostered morale and teamwork among the service members.

WOO: Years later, when I had risen through the ranks and commanded a like unit, I decided to pay a visit on a Friday night to the beloved day room. I asked the one lonely soldier in there, "Where is everyone?" "No one comes here, sir," they are all in their rooms gaming." *What is going on here?* I thought to myself. Social retardation was the answer I eventually came to after observing more behavior. Years ago, one of our inventors on the farm invented a handy little device called a Handy that would drive a nail into the coffin of what was once considered a critical component of social development, conversation. It used to be at the well you would see animals of all types having conversation and communicating. Now all you see is individuals standing around, young and old, staring at their handys. Another area our youth are lacking on is research. Research used to involve looking at several sources in books. Now research is—you guessed it, here comes that handy again—an entry of a question into a search engine and then fixating on a single source as the gospel on a topic. There definitely seems to be a devolving of society on the farm, and I am not sure how to turn it around. Technology has its advantages, but it also has its disadvantages. Automation takes away basic jobs, leaving youth with less opportunity. Artificial intelligence negates the need for individual intelligence.

Where it leads, no one knows. One more thing is today's youth seem unconcerned about history. "Who cares about history, we are the future," chirp the young 'uns, wearing a shirt with a picture of Chewy Gueera, a former terrorist from Brown Land responsible for the death of many innocent animals. When confronted by an older animal as to why they would wear such a shirt portraying such an individual, their response is Chewy was a freedom fighter and besides everyone wears these, it's chic. When asked why they embrace economic systems of the past that had failed over and over, they cannot even explain basic tenets of economics. Their choices seem to be based on mob mentality, and although not the first generation to be anti-establishment, they seem to be on the fast track of disruption. God help our farm, what kind of farm will our children inherit? is what I routinely hear from the older crowd. It is concerning.

ELLIE: What do you think of Sly?

WOO: Well, he's not called *Sly* because he is stupid. He has been running the Red Farm for twenty years and when all is said and done it will be in effect for a quarter of a century. Even when he was in a different position, he transferred powers so that in effect he remained the de facto leader of the farm. Once moving back to the chief position, he simply transferred those powers back to the executive. He also regressed in other areas such as a state-controlled information system on the farm and moving to appoint leaders throughout the farm rather than have them elected.

WOO: Oddly enough, the animals on the Red Farm accepted this. They seem to be animals that are okay with authoritarian leaders. Does that make their system wrong and unacceptable depends on which foxhole you view it from? You can't apply zero-sum analysis when comparing their system to ours. Just because ours is right for us does not mean theirs is wrong for them. I once had

115

the pleasure of a sit-down with Sly, and he had a very interesting analogy when comparing the Rainbow and Red Farms way of conducting business. And I quote, "On the Rainbow Farm you have a very simple game called checkers. We on the other hand play chess. You move a big round piece that can only move one space at a time in a diagonal direction. We have multiple pieces capable of all types of moves. The object of your game is to get as many kings as possible. We have always just one king and protect him to no end. Your big round pieces are always predictable, moving forward. Once they do become a king, their first move is back in the opposite direction. We have several strategies. We can move our little pieces (little green men) who can win a game by themselves through an asymmetrical approach or we can come out heavy with the cavalry, bishops, and rooks, and if need be, our Queen. When you do get on the chessboard, your novice skills become apparent. You abuse your pawns, sacrificing them needlessly. You come out too strong early, leaving gaps in your defenses and, in some cases, leave your King exposed, whether by ignorance or intentionally. Checkers served you well in the past, but those days of simple strategies that worked well in traditional domains such as land, air, and sea are not the calling cards for the new domains of cyber and space. We look forward to the future chess matches we will have with Rainbow Farm in those arenas." Sly continued, "One last point on the one-king system we use to the several-kings systems you use, what you so proudly refer to as checks and balances. In our system, when the king, chief, tsar—whatever you want to call him—says, 'Move the chair to the left side of the room,' the chair instantly gets moved, no questions asked. In your system, your King Executive says, 'Move the chair to the left side of the room.' 'We have a mission,' say all the other kings of the chambers. 'We must look at what the King Executive is proposing. Form a commission immediately to analyze and discuss this very important undertaking of moving a chair.' They immediately form a committee to evaluate the seriousness of this task. Is that the left as we are looking into the room, or is it the left as we are looking from behind the room? Why not move the chair to the middle of the room? Why not slightly off center to the right of the middle? That's not fair—why not off center to the left of the middle? Do we move it to the back or more to the front? Why not paint the chair while we are in discussion on where to move it? Now that it is painted, it fits the right side of the room better. Let's just leave it where it is.

WOO: "So after what should have been a very short time to move a chair went from minutes to hours to days to months. Project Chair ended and is brought to the King Executive to be signed into law. The King Executive is livid. 'I will not pass this law, I will veto it. I asked you simply to move the chair to the left side of the room. All you did was paint the chair, it never moved at all!' So the end result is the chair never moved and more time and energy were spent on painting the chair when that was never in the request in the first place. You call this a system of checks and balances, I call it chaos and a waste of time."

ELLIE: In closing, WOO, what is the one thing that you would like to leave with us?

WOO: That it's not all gloom and doom. We've been here before, not the first time the legitimacy of an elected Chief was put into question. Not the first time we were worried about our youth and the future. Not the first time we have been hopelessly divided. Not the first time for a push for increased government, muzzling of key officials both civilian and military, manufactured news, and falsification of votes at all ruling levels of the farm. The danger that just will not go away is Big Government.

Every time individual animals accept material prosperity in exchange for freedom and individual character, they lose. The Rainbow Farm as shown time and time again its ability to rise above these challenges, internal and external. We will again, and of that I am most certain.

A New Generation on the Farm

Four little rabbits on the far-left side of the garden plot gathered around a head of lettuce. They were the newest representatives of the Donkey Party and had quickly become known as the Darlings of the Donkeys. In secret meetings in the lettuce patch they put their cute little heads together and concocted their own little manifesto, known as the *Iceberg Proclamation*. The unofficial leader of the trio was the cute, agitated orator known as Imperitia. Some of the most outlandish portions of the manifesto was that all the birds that flew and cows like Bessy had to leave the farm. When asked to explain why Imperitia opined *"All Bessie does is fart, she once farted so bad she wilted the leaves on all the lettuce plants."* And in response to flying birds *"What purpose do they serve, all they do is fly around and drop poop, poop from the air, besides who needs to fly, you can hop everywhere you go."*

Imperitia delivers Iceberg proclamation to her squad

Robert. R. Williams is a retired army officer living in Annandale, Virginia. Mr. Williams has a BA in Anthropology from the University of Memphis and a MA in Russian studies from Florida State University.

CPSIA information can be obtained
at www.ICGtesting.com
Printed in the USA
FSHW011219020220
66699FS